Talking With GIANTS! ™

POWERFUL LEADERS SHARE
LIFE LESSONS

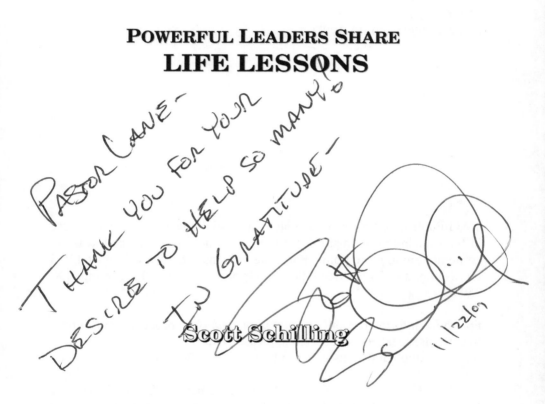

Pastor Cane –
Thank you for your
desire to help so many –
In Gratitude –
[signature] 11/22/09

Scott Schilling

Insight Publishing
Sevierville, Tennessee

ISBN-10:1-60013-172-7
ISBN-13:978-1-60013-172-1

TWG Publishing books are available at special quantity discounts to use in fund raising programs, sales promotions and premiums, or for use in corporate training programs. For more information, please contact TWG Publishing at 4020 N. MacArthur Boulevard, Suite 122-183, Irving, TX, 75038.

For more information on *Talking With Giants!*™ products, consulting, live events, speakers, and services, please visit:
www.TalkingWithGiants.com or phone (972) 659-8941.

Foreword

Talking with Giants!™ is a work that truly comes from the heart—from gratitude—and a true desire to help you feel the successes that come to those who come from a place of service and generosity to others.

Each of us has the capability to achieve whatever we set our minds to accomplish. Many times, it's when we find our higher purpose that the doors start to open up for us personally and professionally.

For years, many toil with our focus on their personal results, only to never really reach the desired result. It is only when we change our mindset and understand that it's when we help others accomplish their desires, our desires get fulfilled.

We live in such a fast-paced society these days, with so much instant gratification that so few initially understand the concepts of doing for others and delayed gratification. The good news is that these are a learned attributes, and when the "student is ready, the teacher will appear."

Hopefully, *Talking With Giants!*™ will awaken your inner desire to give more back to others. While it's true that you certainly will get more by giving—that's still not the reason to give. Don't put any conditions on your giving. As you give unconditionally—of your time, your funds, your love, your support, yourself, you will find riches and blessings beyond your imagination!

Giving is rewarded to levels sometimes beyond comprehension. Lives full of integrity, happiness, love, joy, and prosperity as we live a life of fulfillment—as it has all been intended from the beginning.

To your success!

Scott Schilling

4

Dedication

Talking With Giants![TM] is dedicated to so many who have been true inspirations in my life. Their "servant" hearts are a model of what we should all emulate.

First, to my lovely and beautiful wife, Peggy, who has been my rock through all my endeavors. Peg has supported me no matter what the task or challenge. Her love and support have kept me going, especially in times of difficulty. We've also had so many amazing times together enjoying this gift called life.

To my father, Bill, who for years as I was growing up, selflessly volunteered and spoke on behalf of the United Way, helping to encourage others to contribute, so ultimately they could help so many others.

To my mom, Mary-Jane, who at the ripe young age of eighty-five, recently received recognition for twenty-five years of service as a volunteer for Florida hospitals. She also continues to work forty hours a week and inspires so many others to realize that age is simply a state of mind. And if you want to participate to make this world a better place— all you have to do is engage.

To my sister, Marilyn, who as a neonatal intensive care nurse has worked for years to save lives of infants who, it's hard to believe, could be saved due to size and circumstance.

To my brother, Bruce, who consistently across his lifetime, has worked to invest in people to help give them a better path.

To my son, Taylor, for his amazing heart, light and desire to help others. He is an inspiration with all he has accomplished at such a young age. More importantly, for all the good he will continue to do as he continually learns and grows even more.

To my daughter, Jordan, for her spirit, laughter and "want to" when it comes to anything she decides to accomplish. Jordan is an inspiration because of her desire to help bring those around her up when they need it. She only gets better as she experiences more.

To Jack Canfield for his love, support, guidance and friendship in helping me grow and understand that we all have unlimited potential. That we can accomplish anything we focus our minds on and take action to achieve. And that we can all live lives beyond our current imagination if we truly want to simply "go for it."

And finally, to so many more that they're hard to list: Dr.

5

Fabrizio Mancini, Paul Fulchino, John Dealey, Niki Curry, John Childers, Freddie and Mitzi Rick, Tony O'Donnell, Robert MacPhee, Janet Emerton, Dan Mangini, Dr. Dõv Baron, Michael D'Alessio, the members of my Platinum Mastermind Alliance and Advisory Council, and so many more.

It is with deep gratitude and love that this book is dedicated to those above, and to all people these works might come to touch.

Thank you all for bringing so much into my life and the lives of so many others!

Scott

Table of Contents

Introduction

Talking With Giants!™ has a goal—a goal born out of a burning desire, so powerful that it had to be communicated. Before revealing that goal, I want to share a story with you.

It was late October, 2003, and I was attending *Chicken Soup for the Soul®*, co-creator Mark Victor Hansen's Mega-Speaking event in Los Angeles' massive airport Marriott. The conference is always a phenomenal congress of the most well-known and inspirational public speakers in the country, and this time was no different. Nido Qubin, John Childers, Stedman Graham, Tom Antion—the list seemed endless. All were there!

On the last day of the conference, Cynthia Kersey, renowned for her talks on human potential, was speaking on being individually "Unstoppable." She gave a fabulous talk, and I made copious notes in the back of my already full notebook. As the session was winding down, I began readying my things to move on to the final speaker of the conference. But Cynthia wasn't finished! She began to talk about a cause I had previously only vaguely considered. I found myself drawn back to her voice, so much so that I continued to listen with my briefcase still half open and half packed.

She was seeking support for Habitat for Humanity. Specifically, she hoped to solicit support for the Women's Build Program designed to build homes for homeless families—all constructed by women's hands. Listening intently, I felt an almost overwhelming need grow inside me, the need to support her and the cause she was championing. I had been moved by every speaker at the conference, but it was as if Cynthia was giving me a personal message, and her request would not leave my heart.

I knew I wanted to help, but I was also clearly aware I didn't have the financial resources necessary to support such a project. However, being surrounded by 700 of the speaking industry's biggest and best, inspired me to strive far beyond anything I had done before. Somehow, I was going to help Cynthia with her cause. I just wasn't sure how!

Being from Dallas, I knew many very wealthy and very influential people, but walking up to them with my hand outstretched didn't seem like the answer. There had to be another way!

I went directly from the conference to the airport to catch a red-eye flight back from Los Angeles. After four intensive days of speaker after speaker, I thought I'd be able to sleep on the trip home. But my mind simply wouldn't shut off. It kept cycling through the same feelings and ideas—Cynthia's Habitat for Humanity cause, influential people I knew, my desire to help.

Then, as we flew across country, it struck me! What if I could use the relationships I had with those influential people not only to help Cynthia with her cause, but also help them with the causes they support? What if I could find a way to have them help Cynthia, and in doing so, help others and themselves, all at the same time?

My immediate contribution didn't have to be financial—it could be my time, my talent, and my relationships. It could simply be coming up with an idea stemming from my desire to help and then putting it into action. "Aha!" rang in my ears, drowning out the roar of the engines as the plane set down in the growing dawn light.

Talking With Giants!™ was born!

Cynthia had stirred up in me something that exists in all of us, something that all truly successful people have learned to express—a giving heart!

What I've come to know after interviewing many leaders of their respective industries, is that almost all successful and influential people support some philanthropic cause, and more often than not, several. It's almost a defining characteristic of success: giving to others. These men and women understand that we live in a universe of abundance, and that it's the responsibility of those with wealth and influence to help those in need.

Studying *Giants* across a variety of industries throughout my professional career, it has become very evident that success leaves clues! At some point, each *Giant* has established a direction or goal he or she wanted to achieve, made a decision to get there, created a plan to accomplish it, and then put that plan into action. These giants applied this to both to their personal and professional lives, the process was the same. What may be different from the majority of us, is that they consistently took action and followed through on their plan.

Giants understand another thing quite clearly—giving comes in advance of getting—first not later when we "have more." It is a mindset and heartset that *precedes* success in most cases. It's because of their servant heart that success ultimately blossoms, not the other way around. They live from a place of understanding that *"generosity builds prosperity."*

Many times when people think of giving, they only think of contributing money. While money has the ability to forward many causes, it certainly is not the only thing that can be given to someone in need. Sometimes, money is so easy for some people to give, that it kind of loses any meaning. Far too many people believe that money is the only thing in this world of value. Don't get me wrong, we all need to donate our money and resources to the people, groups, and organizations that do good for so many. The point being made is that it is not the only thing to consider.

In fact, there are many ways to contribute that have nothing to do with money. True *Giants* get out of the mindset that money is the only thing of value that you can donate to help others. Look at Tom Falk the CEO of Kimberly-Clark, a $16 billion company. Tom is a National Trustee for the Boys and Girls Clubs of America (BGCA). Although he personally supports the organization financially, more importantly, he brings his tremendous leadership skills to the BGCA Board that helps direct and grow the organization. These contributions of his expertise and time are priceless!

In most cases, the most precious commodity we have in life is our time. While we all recognize that time is the same for all of us, applying and using that time wisely makes you a *Giant*—no matter what your occupation or station in life. So what should we do with that time? Leverage it! Do the things you can do to achieve

11

multiple successes from the same amount of time and effort.

Jack Canfield is a great example of a *Giant* doing just that. Jack has co-authored the *Chicken Soup for the Soul*® series of books that have sold over 100 million copies to date. That's well over 100 million lives that have been touched by leveraging his efforts. And that's not counting his contributions through his books like *The Success Principles*, his life-changing seminars like *Breakthrough to Success*, or his involvement in movements like those created by *The Secret*. Every one can multiply the effects of their time if they choose to. Do something once, and create a positive impact over and over again.

Giants give of their talents, skills, wisdom, and heart. Trip Kuehne and Art Sellinger use their natural talents in golf to raise money for causes close to their hearts, Juvenile Diabetes and the Autism Society. Both men have family members who have been afflicted with these diseases that need to be understood more fully and hopefully eradicated! Whether performing a demonstration of their golf skills or holding and playing in Pro-Am events, their talents are put to good use. While these are not directly financial contributions, their efforts culminate in raising money from others and have the capability of improving many people's lives.

Another great way to leverage your time is by investing in others through mentoring. No matter who or what you are, there is someone who can benefit from your life experiences. It's not about having reached this pinnacle or that, it's about a heartset of contributing whatever you have at the moment to someone who simply does not have as much. It's pretty simple!

A great example of this is John Dealey. John is selfless when it comes to investing in others—a true giving spirit. His desire to share the wisdom he has gained from so many is amazing! While John has this tremendous knowledge base, it is his desire to pass it along that makes him a *Giant*!

Mentoring creates a sphere of influence that continues far beyond the person you mentored. By helping someone and encouraging them to help someone, who then helps someone, *you can affect world change*. If two help two, who help two and so on, it only takes 32 iterations to cover all 6.4 billion people on our earth—that's amazing!

The universe is constantly expanding. We have the opportunity to help it grow to its full potential. As Jack Canfield said to me a number of years ago, "We've all been put on this earth for only two reasons—to have a fabulous life, and help as many people as we can." Just think if each and everyone of us takes something we know, can do or have, and shares it with others, together, we could improve the lives of so many.

Giants understand this clearly—by giving to others, additional opportunities open up, going forward for all. *Giants* provide solutions to the greatest needs surrounding them. For providing those solutions, they are rewarded with additional leadership opportunities and the other advantages that come with that contribution. Ed Young experienced this by the amazing growth of the Fellowship Church. The formula is simple—give first and then receive the benefits of that generosity, should they show up. Don't wait to receive first before giving.

By the way, there is *always* a benefit to giving. It is not possible to do good for others without feeling a warmth and peace that appears when coming from a heart-felt place of service. Look at the satisfaction Niki Curry derives from helping Orphans Worldwide. The rewards do not have to be material to encourage you to engage. You know when you have done something of value for another—you simply feel it.

The interesting thing is that people, who "in advance" consistently work to help others, seem to enjoy a quality of life that most people desire. Coincidence? I think not! The lessons available from these *Giants* are so numerous, it's hard to detail them all. We can all do so much more than we even believe we can at the outset.

In October of 2003, Cynthia Kersey woke up my desire to give. As I sat and listened to her, I started asking myself how I could best do that. And I kept asking! It was on my flight home that night that the concept of *Talking With Giants!*™ came to me.

The idea behind *Talking With Giants!*™ was simple: cross-pollinate these influential people and their causes, with the goal of furthering them all. Cynthia Kersey's passion to help Habitat for Humanity is immensely powerful, but no less so than the passions of other *Giants,* such as Jack Canfield, Mark Victor Hansen, Ed Young and Dr. Fabrizio Mancini. What started out as an idea to support Cynthia in her plea for Habitat for Humanity, became a realization that we all can do so much more for so many! Thus, the invitation to take action.

What began as a stirring at that conference, became a driving dream at 35,000 feet. More than anything, *Talking With Giants!™* has become a work of the heart. Surrounding myself with the extraordinary people you are about to meet has been a fantastic experience. One that I know will continue to influence me profoundly for the rest of my life.

Hearing the wisdom of these *Giants* has helped me grow in ways I never thought possible. I've seen a side of them most people will never experience—a tremendous opportunity that I can now pass on to you. Beyond their presence and ability to deeply touch so many lives, there is one thing they all share: humility. Time and again, they each spoke of how they would never have been able to accomplish all they had achieved, if they hadn't surrounded themselves with great people! Consistently, they shared that working for the good of others made their own goals even easier to reach.

The people you are about to meet in *Talking With Giants!™* all have what I call a "servant heart." As they have helped others; their own lives and careers have prospered. Perhaps Zig Ziglar said it best many years ago, "You can get everything you want out of life, if you just help enough other people get what they want." This brings us back full-circle to the goal of this book.

This book is written to help you gain some of the amazing insights I have received from reading about and talking with these *Giants.* Hopefully, you to will use these thoughts to help you find your own philanthropic passion! I believe every one of us has the capacity—and therefore the invitation—to help our fellow man. Today, someone needs your time, your wisdom, your talents, and your financial support. My hope is that *Talking With Giants!™*

inspires you to look at how you can give of yourself to help others and in turn, live a much more rewarding and fulfilled life!

To your contributions and ultimate success—

Scott Schilling

Jack Canfield
America's Success Coach

*As the beloved originator of the **Chicken Soup for the Soul**® series, Jack has studied and reported on what makes successful people different. He knows what motivates them, what drives them, and what inspires them. He is a compelling, empowering and compassionate coach who for the past 30 years has helped hundreds of thousands of individuals achieve their dreams.*

SCOTT: Jack, do you realize the impact you have on the people who either listen to you on audio or read your books?

JACK: Occasionally, I get a sense of it. I was recently talking with a young man who is one of the owners of a company called, Dillonas. This man, Dave Morris, was telling me how much I had impacted his life. He was quoting back chapter and verse from my tapes and asking questions about things I haven't written about for at least 10 years.

I think that's just the tip of the iceberg. I have over 2,000 letters on file, and my sister has another 2,000 from teenagers who tell us that because of our *Chicken Soup for the Soul*® books, they did not commit suicide. We get letters from prisoners who say that as a result of reading one of our books, they finally took 100 percent responsibility for their lives.

SCOTT: You've worked with the California Corrections System, welfare recipients, and inner city youth at risk. Why is working with these people such a huge passion for you?

JACK: I've always been attracted to working with people at the lower end of the economic spectrum. I started teaching in an all black inner city high school in Chicago. I have worked with gang members, kids in Job Corps Centers and other places where kids have dropped out or been kicked out of schools.

To be successful and earn a living, they have to have some type of job skills. Some of these kids work to get their GEDs while others learn job skills. It could be as simple as working at a checkout counter in the supermarket, or becoming a cosmetologist. Real life doesn't give them a great path, but all of a sudden, they're making whatever opportunity they get, work.

In particular, I remember a woman I worked with in the Cabrini Green projects in Chicago. She was stuck and couldn't see any way out of her current circumstances. She was a single mom with two kids. How could she ever improve her situation? We came up with the idea of creating what I called a ready-made childcare system. She took another single mom's kids on Tuesdays, Thursdays, and Saturdays, and the other mom took her kids on Mondays, Wednesdays, and Fridays.

Putting that plan into action allowed both of these women to go back to school and get their GEDs. In turn, that allowed them to go to a community college and get their Associate Degrees. By learning some skills, they were able to get jobs and improve their lives economically. They ended up getting out of the projects, off welfare and into their own residences. I believe anybody can do that!

That's the real purpose of welfare, compassion, and philanthropy. There are too many people on welfare who are capable of obtaining and holding down employment. From my experience, they really do want to be employed.

SCOTT: Can you give us an example of this type of situation?

JACK: We were developing our program for the California Welfare System, which now is being used in almost every county in California, and 13 other states. One woman comes to mind in particular. We asked her why she was in our pilot program. She was there voluntarily. She told us she had told her daughter that she had better study because, "You need to get good grades so you can graduate from school." Her daughter answered, "What difference does it make?" The mom asked her, "What will you do if you don't graduate"? Her answer was, "I would go on welfare like you, mom"! The woman said at that moment she realized she was modeling that way of life for her child's future. She didn't want that for her daughter. She realized she had to become the person she wanted her daughter to become.

SCOTT: How do you go from being raised in a small town in rural West Virginia to becoming one of the greatest self-esteem experts of our time?

JACK: Slowly! Seriously, it came from having my own self-esteem issues. As we used to say in graduate school, "If you have an issue, create a curriculum around it." We mostly teach what we need to learn. Dr. John DeMartini said he could always tell what issues I was working on personally, because of the examples I used in my talks.

SCOTT: But how do you get into graduate psychology when you have no undergraduate degrees?

JACK: It is almost impossible. My advisors suggested I go into education because I had already studied history. They felt I could become a history teacher and from there move into psychology through education. So that's what I did. I taught school for a number of years and became far more interested in how to motivate kids than in teaching history. I went back to the University of Massachusetts for my PhD in education with a major in psychology.

There are certain principles everyone needs to know in life. Things like how to negotiate feelings, and how to communicate them effectively so people get their needs met. We all need to manage our own feelings of self-worth and self-esteem, learning to deal with them daily. It's important to set life-planning goals and understand time management. These are the things that really trip people up. Typically, none of these are taught in school.

Anyway, I went from there to training teachers. At one teacher training, someone said that her husband had a company, and he needed this information as badly as teachers did. That scared me because I didn't know anything about business. I thought deep down that the business world wasn't for me—that's why I got into education in the first place.

Nevertheless, I took the risk and worked with that company. I discovered they were just kids who had grown up. They still needed the same stuff that I was trying to get into the high school curriculum. At that point, it was just a matter of packaging it a little differently. Eventually, I found a majority of my work was being done in the corporate world and with professional associations.

SCOTT: Together with Mark Victor Hansen, you have authored over 77 titles and sold almost 100 million *Chicken Soup for the Soul*® books. Can you give us further insight into how it all came about?

JACK: It started one day as I was flying between engagements. Someone asked me if the story I told about this cute little puppy was in a book anywhere. She said, "My daughter really needs to hear that story." I got it from a speech I heard somebody give not long before.

That day, I wrote down a list of about 68 stories. They didn't necessarily even have titles, other than how remembered them in my head. I went home, and began to write up a couple of those stories. Each night I would write a story, then ask my staff to read it and give me feedback. I had about 30 or 40 of the stories written up, saw Mark at a meeting, and we had breakfast together.

Mark asked me what projects I was involved in at that time. I told him I was working on a book. He asked what it was called. I responded, "I haven't decided." Mark said, "What is it about"? I said I was writing a book of inspirational stories without the "you-ought-to's," and "you-shoulda's," and the "how-to's" in between. Something that people can take from the book that hits them personally or individually.

Mark said, "That's a fabulous idea! I want to do that with you." I asked him, "Why would I let you do that? That's like telling James Michener that you'd like to finish *Hawaii* with him when he's halfway finished the book." Mark said, "Because half the stories you stole from me, and second, I have a whole bunch of good stories that you've never even heard."

I said, "Okay, here's the deal. I've got about 68 stories and if you can come up with another 30, I'll let you do the book with me." We figured having about 100 stories would make it easier to get it published, and I like working with somebody because it keeps me accountable and on track. Plus, Mark is a great marketer, a great sales guy, and that would add value to the book and our relationship.

SCOTT: What's your goal for the *Chicken Soup*® series?

JACK: To sell a billion books by the year 2020, and to reach, touch, and positively impact one billion lives.

SCOTT: In another of your books, *The Power of Focus*, you make the claim that you can double a person's income and their time off in less than a year. How can you make that happen?

JACK: The major problem for most people is focus. Their energy goes all over the place because they're responsive to other people's needs rather than being aligned with their own self-chosen goals. When a person gets specific about the behavioral disciplines in *The Power of Focus*, they start producing more results.

We had a group of Realtors go through our training, apply these principles, and within two years, 85 percent of the group had doubled their income and their time off. One person tripled his income in less than a year.

The time off part is actually the easiest to achieve. In the book, there are days we call "free-days"—rest and recreation days. That's defined as a day from midnight to midnight with no work-related activities. By that definition, some people haven't had a day off in years. That means no cell phones, no fax, no business-related reading, no answering your e-mail, no visiting a bookstore if you're writer. You just have to get out of working for that 24-hour period.

There have been studies that show creativity comes from periods where we are well-rested. In our normal scope of activities, our unconscious mind has time to create amazing ideas. An idea like *Chicken Soup for the Soul*® is worth so much more than just giving one more speech. So we encourage people to take at least double the time off they're currently taking.

We ask people to analyze the best day they ever had in their lives, to look at the all the factors involved in that day. Now that I understand that for myself, I can schedule a day full of those types of activities. That's what I know is going to float my boat and give me the juice to come back to work full of energy. I love coming back really ready to go.

To take that time, you only do the most important things that need to get done. You don't get lost in details, and you just get a ton of stuff done. Sometimes you may have to stay up until midnight, but you've got everything done. That's the level of focus we're talking about bringing to the breadth of your work.

SCOTT: Expand on that concept, would you?

JACK: One thing is to be really clear about what you want. Second, break it down into bite size chunks that you can put on your schedule. This is one of things that most people don't do. They don't realize that

21

you have to take your large goals, and get them into whatever system you use to track your day. Then they need to be translated into action steps that have to be taken that day. Just like making a list of errands, like going to the cleaners and shopping, you list the five things that need to be done to achieve your goal by the end of that day.

You also have to measure what you are doing. If you're in sales, you need to measure the number of sales calls. You might start by first measuring the number of appointments that are set. Then, determine the ratio of sales to appointments. Once you have these numbers, you can look at how to make those ratios more efficient.

Having an accountability partner is also very important. This is someone who's going to hold you accountable, whether it's a coach, a mentor, a partner or mastermind alliance. If you and I were in an accountability relationship, we would spend time talking about your goals for the following week. You would tell me what you're going to get accomplished by next week, and I would tell you what I'll accomplish by next week. On Friday, at 4:00PM of each week, I know we're going to be reviewing the week. If by Thursday, I have not accomplished what I suggested to you I would, I'd get busy. No one ever wants to tell their partner that they didn't get something done that they had committed to accomplish.

SCOTT: You co-authored a work called, *In Defense of Self-Esteem*. How did that come about and why is it important?

JACK: Self-esteem is an incredibly important thing. I refer to it as having a stack of poker chips. If you have 10 poker chips, and I have 100, and we play poker together, you're likely to play more cautiously because you only have 10 chips. I can take bigger risks than you can.

Life is like poker in that you have to take risks at times to be successful. Kids in school won't raise their hand if they think someone will make fun of them. If they have low self-esteem, they sit in the back of the room. They don't participate in conversations because they don't want to say something dumb. There's an old phrase that says, "It's better to stay quiet and have people think you the fool than to open up your mouth and remove all doubt." That was one of the things that I grew up hearing. "Nothing risked, nothing gained," but also "Nothing risked, nothing lost"! Other than, of course, you lose the opportunity to achieve. I've always been a huge advocate of the importance of self-esteem.

As I said earlier, I enjoy working with people at the lower end of the economic spectrum in part, because they often have low self-esteem. I've seen lifting or raising their self-esteem work over and over with lives transformed!

Unfortunately, currently there are people in the academic world talking about how self-esteem is a bad thing. They really don't understand it. There are some people who misuse the term, doing things like giving every kid an "A" grade for no effort. That's ridiculous! I was a member of the California Task Force for Self-Esteem, and Personal and Social Responsibility. We took a lot of teasing about how it was a touchy-feely "California thing." But we came up with some powerful research about the effects of low self-esteem and drug abuse, pregnancies, dropouts, low grades and other factors. All these things are related to success in life. There are even studies showing that people with low self-esteem get sick more often. There's something called psychoneuroimmunology, which says your attitude affects your nervous system and ultimately your health.

SCOTT: You claim that social epidemics like drug abuse, school violence, adolescent suicide, and depression are, for the most part, the result of low self-esteem. Can you expand on this for us?

JACK: I define self-esteem as being lovable and capable. If I feel worthy of happiness, I am worthy of love, and I also have other people who love me and want me to pursue my own pleasure and happiness. In low self-esteem situations, we see an increase in drug use because that person does not feel that his feelings are okay. He doesn't have the skills necessary for reaching out and building relationships, or dealing with the sting of rejection. Therefore he turns to drugs and alcohol to numb the pain.

In my seminars, I will ask certain people if there's a reason they haven't raised their hand. Their typical answer is that their problems are not that important, or that other people's problems are more worthy of being talked about. These people feel they're not worthy of taking up the group's time. A lot of people suffer in silence.

SCOTT: What are the signs of high self-esteem?

JACK: People are happy. They pursue their own goals. They have boundaries. They're able to say no to that which they don't want to do. They say yes to that which they want. They're fully alive! They have a lot of energy. They have charisma, and they're not depressed. They tend to be more cooperative because they're not trying prove anything to anybody. They're not covering up low self-esteem by being a jerk. They're more collaborative and more creative. Their humor typically does not put other people down, nor is it sarcastic, which is really veiled anger. They're healthy, vibrant, and purposeful. They keep their word, do what they say they're going to do. They won't overwhelm themselves. These are some of the solid characteristics of high self-esteem.

SCOTT: If somebody has low self-esteem, what exercises could they use to increase their self-esteem?

JACK: I've put together two audio albums. One is called, "Self-Esteem and Performance," and the second is called, "Maximum Confidence." Between the two, there are somewhere between 30 and 50 specific techniques that you can do to develop your self-esteem. They include therapy, counseling, coaching, and getting a third party to assist you in expressing your feelings and focusing your mind. Also, use positive affirmations.

I also believe that surrounding yourself with positive people and reading uplifting books increase your self-esteem. The other part of that is staying away from people who are negative and can bring you down.

SCOTT: Which cause you would like to call to everyone's attention?

JACK: I think everyone should find a cause that sings to them, because then you're doing what you have a passion for. I have a passion for literacy because I'm someone who loves to read and write books. It hurts me to think about people who can't read, because they can never take advantage of great literature, or "how-to books" that can solve many of their problems. Literacy is one cause I support tremendously!

Another is anything that helps support the reduction of violence against children. In my own town, there's an organization called CALM—Child Abuse Listening and Mediation—and every year we have a fund-raising event during which we bring together four authors. Last year we had Steven J. Cannell, who is one of the great Hollywood writers. We've had folks like Jonathan Winters and other wonderful people who have contributed their support and money to that organization.

Mark and I are very proud that with every one of our *Chicken Soup*® books, we've donated a portion of the profits to a cause related to the topic of the book. For one book, we picked Habitat for Humanity. For another book, we thought we should replant trees because of all the paper we were using, so we were responsible for planting a million trees in Yosemite. We've done charities related to cancer, and to animals for the pet lover's book. We also work with the Make-A-Wish Foundation because, again, we're very committed to kids.

SCOTT: What last pearl of wisdom would you like to pass along?

JACK: What I've been learning most recently, which is extremely exciting to me, is that we're all working too hard to manifest that which we want to see manifested in our life. I've always known this, but I've never known it quite at the level I do today. It's kind of my quest to understand it fully.

The quality of our being is what attracts people to us. The idea is that we cannot attract into our life that which is not vibrating at the same level we are. For example, we could want more abundance in our life, but we're vibrating how poor we are, so we attract more poverty. But you and I have both met people who didn't have a lot of money, but had tremendous abundance in their life. It's in the beauty that nature brings them, the joy they get from their children and their work. Mother Teresa had no personal possessions, yet she could get anything she wanted any time she wanted from anybody she wanted. No one would ever deny her. She literally got wars to stop for a day so she could pull children out of a war zone. She got Rudy Giuliani to personally handle about 15 permits in one day, which would have normally taken months, so she could build a Sisters of Charity building that would take care of sick people in New York. She came from a state of abundance even though she had nothing personally. And it's because she had nothing but felt like she had everything. As a result, everything was attracted to her.

She's always been my ideal, someone to look up to as an ideal model. It is the quality of her consciousness that was so amazing. The reality is we all have that available to us if we'll simply become that which we want to be. We need to put ourselves in a place of abundance, a place of gratitude, a place of "your way," and do those things that make our hearts feel good. So many people are working so hard, and feeling so bad about working hard, that with the bad feelings they're pushing away the very things that they want to attract into their lives.

SCOTT: Thank you so much for your insight, wisdom, friendship, and guidance.

- To help support ProLiteracy Worldwide, obtain information and make donations, please contact http://www.proliteracy.org, or call Toll Free: 888-528-2224.
- To help support CALM, obtain information and make donations, please contact http://calm4kids.org, or call 805-965-2376.
- To reach Jack, contact him at www.JackCanfield.com or www.ChickenSoupfortheSoul.com.

Mark Victor Hansen
America's Ambassador of Possibilities

Mark Victor Hansen is known to most people as the co-creator of the mega best-selling Chicken Soup for the Soul® *book series. But in reality, Mark's ventures range far and wide beyond these popular books. He's working to create a more enlightened society by teaching people how to become "enlightened millionaires," to develop their sense of vision, and to create a system to help them achieve success. He's even taking on the twin monsters of homelessness and illiteracy. Obviously, this son of Danish immigrants is a man worth meeting.*

SCOTT: Mark, you made a very interesting statement to me in a recent conversation. You said that as individuals, if we don't maximize our potential we are actually being selfish, because we're cheating the world of our humanitarian participation. Can you expand on that?

MARK: There is interesting new research coming out of the Scalar Waves Center, run by Dr. Mick Hall. He takes pictures of people's blood cell analysis and shows that approximately 35 percent are alive, but after Scalars, 100 percent are alive. He's going to be testing at my seminars because he's finding that we're working far below our potential. In the old days, Earl Nightingale said we only use five percent of our potential, and today's psychologists say we're only using 10 percent. What I'm saying is if we're all under-using our potential, the way to release it is to decide what you're passionately purposed about, visualize it, take ownership of it, and put together a team. By the way, my acronym for TEAM is Together Everyone Accomplishes Miracles.

SCOTT: You are a passionate philanthropist and humanitarian. What are the main causes you support?

MARK: Every one of the *Chicken Soup*® books is tied to a philanthropic cause. There are 77 of them (at press time) through which we've donated over $7 million. My number two cause right now, because of *The One Minute Millionaire*, is creating one million millionaires that all give away a million dollars to their church or philanthropic cause.

Only half those people go to a church, synagogue, or mosque, so the other half will give it to a charity that they care about. For example, I

27

heard from a guy who had been a physician's assistant and had a terrible accident and wound up in a wheelchair, unable to work. Six months later after he heard me he was making $15,000 a month, and he gave away 26 wheelchairs to people who needed them.

Being a visionary is a high spiritual calling. The hard job is getting the front end going and seeing how this works. The easier side of the job is to organize a team and get them together, and then make it happen to levels of success that nobody thought were achievable, for a mutual positive good.

SCOTT: This idea came directly from conversations we had together talking about my vision.

MARK: Isn't that cool? Cynthia Kersey and I are now raising $275 million to build 30,000 houses for Habitat for Humanity. What's happened as a result of that is that I'm sharing that vision with my partners, just like what you said. That's what it takes—figure out what you're going to do and the ways and means become available.

SCOTT: How did you get involved with the American Red Cross?

MARK: We made the decision that we wanted to give to the American Red Cross, so Leeza Gibbons and William Shatner and I were the spokespersons. We were in Washington, D.C., and we did the things we could do, making a number of different appeals. There was a situation not long ago where the country was virtually almost all out of blood for transfusion, so we made an appeal to the chiropractic industry. About half of the chiropractic industry, about 30,000 chiropractors, brought bloodmobiles to their locations and their patients donated blood. We also asked each patient to bring along a friend. I think we ended up with about 330,000 pints of blood in a week's time.

While I was in Washington, DC, I discovered that only five percent of us ever give blood. I also discovered that there's a thing called a ten-gallon giver. At the time my partners weren't involved, so my wife and I decided we would build a Ten Gallon Givers Wall to recognize those who've donated 10 gallons of blood. We're still working out the politics of it with the American Red Cross but it's something we have a desire to do. You can give blood once every 56 days and once you've given the equivalent of 10 gallons of blood, potentially you have saved

1,000 lives of people you'll never meet. That is just so cool I can't believe it.

SCOTT: You have written *The Miracle of Tithing* and I find it fascinating. Why did you write it?

MARK: Because I'm a passionate believer in giving back 10 percent or more. It's not a human commandment, it's a spiritual commandment, and it goes through every spiritual system. Somebody who's critical and cynical and negative and obtuse is going to say that's just so we can get a church founded. I suppose that's true, but spiritual work needs to be paid with spiritual money.

In tithing, if you get ten cents, you donate a penny of it, every time. Now, most people say, "I'll do that when I get a million dollars, then I'll give a hundred thousand." But that's too late! You have to give what you're growing. If you keep doing that, the doors thrust open at levels you can't believe. You get to meet people, even old people like me, and all you need to do is show off this wonderful thing that you're doing.

SCOTT: I don't know of anyone who's better at bringing people together than you. Have you been told that?

MARK: I'm told that I'm pretty good at that. Here's a perfect example—John Childers and I are putting together a company where we teach people how to network. In fact, we help them create their network with extremely influential, high-end participants. We are going to go to exotic places and meet celebrities. It's going to be really big. And John is figuring out how to run the whole company. We've come together because I've got this little skill of meeting and growing relationships, and John understands how to monetize that. It's going to be called WINGS, Wealth International Network Group.

SCOTT: What a way to get things accomplished by associating with the best of the best!

MARK: The point is that we all come together. When you have a group of this magnitude together, they'll sit at the front of their chairs. They pay attention, and they'll usually decide to get some stuff done together for the common good. If we do that, we can change the world! Why not have people pay to participate in an activity that can change the world? I don't think there's anything wrong with that.

SCOTT: What drives you to work so hard?

MARK: Mainly because I really enjoy it. I enjoy talking to you. I enjoy talking to Dr. Fabrizio Mancini, who I know is going to be part of this book. This is the kind of thing I love to spend my day doing. I've been on calls to Fab almost daily talking about the upcoming Parker (College of Chiropractic) seminar in Las Vegas. John Childers is holding a seminar that same weekend with about 100 people. We're going to invite those 100 people to come over and experience what the Parker seminars have to offer. More than likely, those people will become instantaneous advocates of the chiropractic wellness movement. They've probably never seen 10,000 chiropractors together and have never shared the good that they can accomplish. With that, they're going to get enrolled at a level like no one else. After that, Parker is going to invite the public to attend so they can share in the excitement.

SCOTT: You are billed as America's Ambassador of Possibility. What does that mean to you?

MARK: Success is creating a state of mind which allows you to achieve whatever it is that you want. We all have infinite possibilities within. I do what I can to help people recognize how wonderful they really are.

SCOTT: With your Business partner Jack Canfield, you've created what Time magazine calls "the publishing phenomenon of the decade with your *Chicken Soup for the Soul®* series. How did you make it happen?

MARK: We were turned down by many publishing houses, even though we thought we had something that was a real winner. Jack and I made the decision that this was going to be a success, and in doing so we set out a plan to do a least five things every day to further the efforts of getting the book published and sold.

We constantly contacted those people who saw any potential of selling the book and enlisted them in our dream. And so far, we've sold over 100 million *Chicken Soup for the Soul®* books in North America alone, and we have over 100 licensed products in the marketplace. *Chicken Soup*® is one of the most successful publishing enterprises in America today.

SCOTT: You recently came out with *The One Minute Millionaire: The Enlightened Way to Wealth*. What is the enlightened way?

MARK: Everybody wants the freedom of lifestyle that prosperity can create. Together with Bob Allen, I've worked to unlock the actions and attitudes you need to gain the abundance you want in your life. We help you discover them by changing your thinking and expectations, and by recognizing that giving to others can be one of the greatest assets in your journey to wealth and prosperity.

The universe is fundamentally abundant. There is no shortage except for consciousness. There are 24 principles of wealth abundance and prosperity identified in, *The One Minute Millionaire*. I've discovered through a lifetime of tithing that giving does not cause you to have less but in fact guarantees that ultimately you will have more.

SCOTT: Together with Jack Canfield and Les Hewitt, you wrote the book *The Power of Focus*. What can you tell us about the power of focus?

MARK: Many times people are totally overwhelmed by their surroundings and circumstances. The number one reason that stops people from getting what they want is a lack of focus. But we can give a person the strategy necessary for them to achieve that focus. We work on getting past old patterns of procrastination and other habits that keep you from achieving your desired results. The power of focus helps you shift from feeling overwhelmed to the creation of an easy and effective action plan by consciously focusing on the desired results.

SCOTT: Not long ago I read the *Aladdin Factor*, which you also wrote with Jack Canfield. I can't tell you how many times I've put the power of asking into effect. Is it true that anything is possible if you dare ask?

MARK: If you want to G-E-T you need to A-S-K! Far too often people settle for lives that are ordinary. We haven't learned to ask for what we want or for some reason we feel we don't deserve it. Everyone truly knows what they want, but because of fear, guilt, or maybe limiting beliefs, we're stopped from asking for it. *The Aladdin Factor* helps clear that picture so that you can build your self-esteem, your self-reliance, and the ability to make a difference.

SCOTT: In the seminar you're giving, you talked about a BHAG. What's a BHAG?

MARK: A Big Hairy Audacious Goal! It's when you set a goal that's absolutely huge! It does a couple of things. It inspires people to want to join you. Second, it forces you to grow and achieve. Jack and I created a goal—to sell a billion books. That's a BHAG!

Beyond setting your BHAG, everyone needs to set at least 101 goals. You should be scared and thrilled all at the same time. If you write those goals down, they will manifest themselves. When you ask the mind a question, it has no choice but to work on a solution. In reality, your state of mind creates the state of result.

SCOTT: What final bit of wisdom would you like to pass along?

MARK: You have to take control of your thinking, tell yourself how to feel, and then feel that way so you can literally ordain your destiny. When you make your destiny better, success is the most unselfish thing you do, because God said, "The greatest amongst you is servant of all." If we start serving at higher, bigger, better, more dynamic and passionate levels, everybody's going to get it. We can push back against poverty. Half of the planet is illiterate. Many more are starving. If you change your consciousness, which is what I'm all about, then you've ordered a change in your personal result and the results of the future.

- To help support the American Red Cross, obtain information and make donations, go to www.redcross.org, or call 800-REDCROSS.
- To help support Habitat for Humanity, obtain information and make donations, go to www.habitat.org, or call 229-924-6935.
- To learn more about Mark, go to www.markvictorhansen.com.

Cynthia Kersey
Becoming Unstoppable

Can you change your life in 30 days? Cynthia Kersey says you can. Her approach to change, a one-day-at-a-time regimen detailed in her book, Unstoppable, *reflects her own belief in herself and her ability to escape an unfulfilling path by sheer will. Now, she talks about how she's sharing her wisdom with women all over the world.*

SCOTT: Your personal story proves that everyone can be really unstoppable! Give us some of your history.

CYNTHIA: I was raised in Cincinnati, Ohio. My mom and dad worked for Procter & Gamble for 30 years. They were not risk takers, nor am I. I was really encouraged by my parents to maintain the status quo. Basically their word of advice for me was that I needed to get a good job, and I needed to get a good husband. I literally went to college to find a good husband.

SCOTT: To get that MRS. Degree!

CYNTHIA: Yeah! And then follow in my mother's footsteps. I went to college and got married before I graduated. I ended up graduating later. I had my husband, and we then had a baby. I was a secretary and not that great at it. I was fired from my first job, and demoted from my second. Then, I interviewed at Sprint and was hired as an entry-level telemarketer. Within weeks I became the number-one performer in a section of 52 telemarketers. That was a big turning point for me! Actually that was the first time I had done something I was really great at. From my point of view, I was just making friends on the phone. It didn't feel like work to me.

I went back to school, I got my degree, and I became a student of peak performance—the principles that enable ordinary people to really create amazing results in their lives. As I followed their examples, I had even more success at Sprint. I sold a contract worth over $30 million to Kinko's, and that became the first national retail video conferencing network.

SCOTT: But you weren't really satisfied, were you?

33

CYNTHIA: No. I had made it to the top in the telecommunications industry, yet I wasn't passionate about what I was doing. I was happy that I had achieved that success, but not passionate about telecommunications. I started this journey to claim what would give my life meaning, what would be exciting to me. I realized I personally had something that I had always known throughout my whole life. "Cynthia" means reflector of light. And I realized that what excited me the most was to encourage people—to be a source of light, to be a source of encouragement and love. I decided that I wanted to write a book. I had no experience in that, had never written anything more than a college term paper, and knew no one in the business. But I did my research, and within weeks after making that decision we had downsized our life, and I had cashed in my life savings to write and publish a book.

SCOTT: That was *Unstoppable*?

CYNTHIA: Yes. I left Sprint in January 1996, and the book was published March 1998.

SCOTT: I know that you had some adversity along the way. What made you go forward, versus staying down?

CYNTHIA: There is adversity in life all the time. When you're an unpublished author, you're one of a sea of many people who want to be published, right?

SCOTT: Correct.

CYNTHIA: You're not being taken seriously, not being able to get interviews, struggling financially—I was living off my savings to write the book. I ran into all sorts of naysayers, people who said, "You're quitting your job to do *what*"? It's hard getting the momentum to do something different. The thing that kept me going was my purpose. I love this! I wanted to make a difference, to feel like my life was contributing to others, and I really wanted to share the information that had made such a profound impact on my life. The possibility of living that as a career was very exciting to me! I put everything on the line. I risked everything. I felt like my family was in it as well, and I felt that I couldn't let them down. I had a strong purpose, and a compelling reason to make it happen.

SCOTT: You spent a lot of years researching some of the greatest achievers. What things did you find that they had in common?

CYNTHIA: In my first book I really talk about the "Seven Characteristics of Unstoppable People." Those are the key things I think they have in common. There's a "bigness" to them, a "bigness" of them—in living and giving and being and contributing. They're just like us, but they see things in a bigger way, and they don't let their own limitations stop them.

SCOTT: They all seem to abolish any self-limiting beliefs.

CYNTHIA: And those beliefs are always there. I'm sure these people deal with them as well, but they don't let the limits stop them. They're focused on what they're doing, they have a purpose, they're passionate, and they believe anything is possible.

SCOTT: What kind of impact would you like to see your *Unstoppable* books make?

CYNTHIA: Well you know, I just published *Unstoppable Women*, and I'm doing three other books, with *Unstoppable Courage*, being the first. I'm going to publish a line of *Unstoppable Courage* books. I've got a lot of things going. My vision is to inspire people to live unstoppable lives. I'm working to inspire women to commit to creating unstoppable moments. Anybody can take the time to create an unstoppable moment.

SCOTT: What's an unstoppable moment?

CYNTHIA: An unstoppable moment is making five more phone calls when you want to quit. It's eating a grapefruit or something healthy when you would rather have a Twinkie. It's getting your butt off the couch and walking for 30 minutes when you'd rather sit and watch reality television. All of those moments add up. There are decisions that we can make every day that will ultimately transform us.

35

SCOTT: What's the value of creating an unstoppable moment?

CYNTHIA: When you create a series of them, ultimately it creates an unstoppable life. My vision is to create awareness and a desire within people that being unstoppable isn't something that's only for the few, but that they can do it every day in their family, or their health, or their fitness.

SCOTT: Well, I've just pulled off the side of the road, and I was thinking, "I wonder if I'll have an ice cream cone after we're done here"? You just changed my mind.

SCOTT: What has been the response to the book?

CYNTHIA: It's interesting, because before my book came out, I felt almost desperation to have my life count. When I was in Corporate America, my life was all about me and my family. But getting into this work has transitioned me to a much higher purpose. I feel like I'm contributing. I get letters, phone calls, and e-mails every day from people who tell me how this has inspired them to do all sorts of things. People want hope, and that's what this is. I just want to continue to get the message out through additional books, speaking, and other things.

SCOTT: What's your definition of a meaningful life?

CYNTHIA: It's knowing what you love, and finding a way to express that in the world.

SCOTT: That's a great definition.

CYNTHIA: I need to go write that down!

SCOTT: Who are your mentors?

CYNTHIA: Well, the most significant mentor in my life has been Millard Fuller, the founder of Habitat for Humanity. He has been the most profound, because his life represents true spirituality, which is love in action. His intention is so pure. He is an unstoppable man, whose vision is to eliminate poverty housing from the face of the earth. He started Habitat almost 30 years ago, building one house in rural Georgia. Now they've built over 100,000 homes, housed almost a million people, and it just continues! His life is so rich, but he really doesn't have that much money. He's one of the lowest paid CEOs of a nonprofit of its size, a billion dollar nonprofit. But he's one of the richest people in the world.

He's important to me because I want to contribute and express love in tangible ways, and I think he is a great model. And he has always believed in me. When I first met him, I had just written my manuscript. I interviewed him, and he saw something in me I didn't even see in myself. He has been an encouragement and an example of what I want to be in the world.

SCOTT: At Mark Victor Hansen's Mega Speaking seminar, you and Mark talked about Habitat, and the Women's Build program which was amazing to me. How did you get involved?

CYNTHIA: First off, I have an intimate knowledge of Habitat because of my friendship with Millard. My first project with them was after I had separated from my husband. That January, Millard had just gotten back from Nepal. And after spending the holidays with my mom and dad, feeling so miserable, and being devastated by going through divorce, I wanted to do something for somebody else. Like Millard says, "We become wounded healers." Everybody has pain, and if we can use that pain to do good, we become the beneficiary of that good.

SCOTT: That's a wonderful idea.

CYNTHIA: He suggested, "Well, why don't you raise some money and build a couple of houses in Nepal"? As I've said before, when you have great pain in your life, you need a greater purpose. And I thought, "How many homes would I need to build to offset this pain in my life"? When I got to 100, that felt bigger than my pain. I had never raised money or been to Nepal, but that purpose kept me going through the most difficult year of my life. I ended up raising $200,000. We took 18 people to Nepal and started building 100 homes. Then when I spoke about it, another company said, "Well, we have a large constituency in South America." We raised money to build homes in Guatemala. And with *Unstoppable Women,* I wanted to do something for women. I talked to Habitat's Women's Build Department, and now I've already raised $500,000 of the two million dollars that will go to build homes for 40 moms and their kids, worldwide.

SCOTT: Does your passion come from trying to beat the hurt?

CYNTHIA: Not any more. It did then, but I was trying to fulfill a purpose. What drives me now is to make a difference. I want to contribute. I want to make a difference in people's lives.

SCOTT: You also formed the Unstoppable Foundation. What's its mission?

CYNTHIA: It's about creating tools to empower women and children around the world. I think women are the mothers of the world. And if we don't do it, who is going to do it? It's how we're built.

SCOTT: How do you encourage more women who are not just captains of industry but stay-at-home moms?

CYNTHIA: I think it goes back to helping people get in touch with their purpose. If you're a stay-at-home mom, your purpose is to raise healthy, happy children. My work is really about helping people stay focused on, "How can I do that? What's one thing that I could do to be better at it every day"? Whatever anybody's path in life is, or wherever they are in their lives, I think my purpose is to help them get back to what is important to them, to rediscover what they value. Then help them learn how to express that in the world. If you're a mom, be the best mom you could be. Be an unstoppable mom! If you want to add something else, you add something else.

SCOTT: Is that really the unstoppable mindset?

CYNTHIA: For me, it's all about creating a life of meaning. Being unstoppable is having a purpose, having the courage to make a change in your life, and to go for something, then not to let your own limitations or circumstances stop you. Each step toward that is an unstoppable moment. These moments create your path. I like breaking it down into things that everybody can relate to.

SCOTT: How do you enlist people to live from their hearts?

CYNTHIA: I just think you speak from your own truth. I think when the student's ready, the teacher will appear. When I speak, when people are open and receptive, no explanation is necessary for those who get it. For those who don't, no explanation is possible. When I'm out there speaking, I'm speaking my message, my truth. I'm just living my truth in a way that works for me, and I express it. This works for me. This inspires me! When it resonates for other people and they respond, that's great! And if they don't, that's okay too.

SCOTT: That's great. You do corporate training, workshops, and the like. What do you want people to walk away with from these events when you're done?

CYNTHIA: I want them to walk away with a greater recognition of what they can do and be. How they can contribute, how they can give, how they can be more. If people can walk away with an increased recognition of who they are, what's possible, and how they can be unstoppable in making a change, I'm thrilled. So many people struggle. So many people give up. So many people give in, and it damages their psyche. It damages their confidence. It makes them feel that they're not worthy. And that's not true. It's about just doing one thing and building on that success, as opposed to biting off more than you can chew and trying to change eight things in a week. Research indicates that people can't change 10 things at once. Focus on one thing, and create success in that area. That success is a foundation that can transform everything.

SCOTT: Is there one last idea that you really want to pass along to everybody?

CYNTHIA: You know, I think the bottom line is, when you find something that's meaningful, be unabashed about it. It may not look like A, B, C or D, but it's your way. And when you find it, and you accept it, and you step into it, there's a lot of power in living in your own truth, and being authentic. And I think that's really where the joy is. People deserve—they owe it to themselves—to get clear on what that would be. You know, what is their uniqueness, and how can they express it in a way that it's exciting to them.

SCOTT: Is finding that uniqueness and then putting it into play what creates that resonant passion?

CYNTHIA: Absolutely! You've got a purpose, and then you find a way to express it in the world. That's exactly how I would define passion.

SCOTT: That's a great definition of taking your individual talents and using them for a greater good.

CYNTHIA: Definitely. Because it's not just something you love, but it's tied into something that's bigger than you.

SCOTT: What I've found to be interesting in talking to all the people I've interviewed is their humility. They all ask, "Why do you consider me a giant? I'm just a person"!

CYNTHIA: Right!

SCOTT: The reality is that they're a person who's providing a tremendous amount of inspiration.

CYNTHIA: Exactly. I thought the same thing when I interviewed people for *Unstoppable Women.* I met all these amazing women, but they don't see themselves as being amazing.

SCOTT: That's an interesting dynamic that seems to be very consistent.

CYNTHIA: I think it's because they're just doing what they love. If people start believing their own press, they get annoying.

SCOTT: I've seen some very successful people with some very big egos, and they are a pain to be around. But the people who endure tend to be the ones with great success but small egos.

CYNTHIA: I think Mark Victor Hansen and Jack Canfield are perfect examples of that.

SCOTT: I agree. I actually asked Jack how it feels to impact as many lives as he has. And he said, "I don't necessarily recognize that I've done that, unless somebody specifically comes up and talks to me. I just think I'm Jack, writing a book"!

CYNTHIA: Yeah. Exactly right!

SCOTT: I truly do appreciate your doing this with me, Cynthia. I think it's going to be a wonderful project to help a lot of people.

CYNTHIA: Well, thank you for persevering. A lot of people talk about doing things, and you're doing it. I congratulate you on taking the action. You're already unstoppable. It's just a matter of continuing to go down the path and just get it done.

- To help support Habitat for Humanity, obtain information and make donations, go to www.habitat.org, or call 229-924-6935.
- To support the Unstoppable Foundation, obtain information and make donations, please contact: http://unstoppable.net/foundation.asp or call 888-867-8677.
- To learn more about Cynthia go to: www.unstoppable.net.

Dr. Fabrizio Mancini
Chiropractor on a Mission

Dr. Fabrizio Mancini is one of the most amazing people I know. "Fab" was born in Colombia to a Colombian mother, Gladys, and Italian father, Giovanni. Fab's desire was originally to become a neurosurgeon, and in 1978, he moved to the United States to begin pursuing his dream. In 1987, he discovered the chiropractic profession and enrolled at Parker College of Chiropractic. Fabrizio recognized the potential for preventing disease through chiropractic versus treating the results of disease. His vision of lifetime wellness through chiropractic care began to form. In 1999 at age 33, Fabrizio became one of the youngest college presidents in the nation as he took the lead at Parker College. With clarity of vision, Fab has enlisted and engaged a "dream team" of industry giants to forever change the way chiropractic is viewed—to refine the vision of a wellness lifestyle and chiropractic's role in leading this movement.

Fab has authored numerous articles in the chiropractic industry and beyond, and co-written Chicken Soup for the Chiropractor's Soul®. *He is an internationally renowned speaker, an educator, president of Parker Seminars the largest wellness seminar provider in the world, and a healer, humanitarian, and philanthropist with a heart the size of Texas.*

SCOTT: Fab, thank you for taking the time to share your vision.

FABRIZIO (FAB): Thank you; it's a pleasure to able to share some of the things we are doing to help promote the wellness revolution.

SCOTT: How have you seen the role of the chiropractor changing in today's health care system?

FAB: We are noticing today that the incoming student is a different student than came into the profession even ten years ago. The industry is attracting a lot of younger individuals, a lot more females, and many more people who are interested in a lifestyle of wellness. The profile of today's student is that most of them are very fit, very clean cut, and eat very healthy. The biggest thing is their passion and desire to serve humanity by passing along the things they value, like living a healthy lifestyle.

SCOTT: It sounds like they are coming into Parker learning to talk the talk, but many are already walking the walk.

FAB: That's the thing that gets me so excited about the future. In the past, many of the people who came into the profession were not the healthiest individuals. In fact, most of them were very analytical and intelligent, but as you know, your actions speak louder than your words. The patients themselves are being very critical of the advice being given about nutrition, health, or changes in their lifestyle. They look at the actions of the person giving the advice, and many times it is inconsistent with the suggestions. If so, that person quickly loses credibility.

Now the people coming into the profession are aware they need to model the proper behaviors. Because of that, we will be able to communicate the benefits of a healthy lifestyle much more effectively, because it's no longer just words, it can be seen in their actions.

SCOTT: Earlier you said that there were more and more women entering the chiropractic profession. How do you see the numbers changing?

FAB: At Parker College, women now make up 28 percent of our enrollment. In chiropractic overall, women make up just over 40 percent of the total, and it is estimated that it will reach a 50/50 balance in the next 10 years. We've found in the industry that women bring some very valuable attributes to the profession—one being so sensitive to what the patients are experiencing. At the same time, they demonstrate a great ambition to help others live a healthy lifestyle. I believe this nature is changing not only in chiropractic, but in other health disciplines as well.

SCOTT: With the movement toward alternative health care and especially chiropractic, how has enrollment at Parker College been impacted?

FAB: The Department of Labor recently came out with some new statistics stating that currently chiropractic is the fastest growing healthcare profession, and is expected to continue that way until 2010. People are looking for the "great jobs of the future" and chiropractic comes to the forefront. Another study shows that chiropractic ranks as the second healthiest profession to be in, meaning that the practitioners themselves are healthier. A Harvard study looked at the people who seek alternative or holistic medicine. Visits to chiropractic practitioners out-numbered all other holistic disciplines put together.

There is definitely a movement toward conservative, natural, and holistic professionals to guide people toward greater health. Additionally, many people are asking their caregivers to become more active in their healthcare—not just telling them what to do, but showing them, guiding them toward making better decisions.

Because of this, our enrollment growth has been tremendous. This year we have had a 15 percent gain, and we see that potentially doubling next year. This is very exciting. It's obvious the awareness of chiropractic is growing, and it seems we are communicating more effectively to those candidates who are looking for a career change. Also, we are attracting other individuals who are in school right now and struggling to make a decision about their future. Many more are definitely considering chiropractic as a profession because of the tremendous benefits the profession has to offer.

SCOTT: Earlier you mentioned families in chiropractic care as another change you've seen in recent years.

FAB: In the past, chiropractic was looked at as providing symptomatic relief, much like mainstream medicine. You see, we really don't have a healthcare system, we have a disease care system. By that I mean a patient must already have some problem before they seek help for that problem. The premise of chiropractic is one of preventive care by checking the body to ensure that it is properly functioning in order to prevent disease from happening in the first place. Chiropractic is not simply there to relieve symptoms once a problem arises.

Today's chiropractic movement is introducing the wellness concept to the entire family. It's not just for adults who have backaches due to playing golf or wrist pain because of being at the computer too long. Chiropractic Practitioners are finally taking the time to educate their patients to bring their children, parents, and grandparents in for treatment.

SCOTT: Along with your beautiful wife, Alicia, you have two boys, Gianni and Luciano. How soon after they were born did they receive their first chiropractic adjustment?

FAB: The amazing thing is that for both of them, it was almost instantly! As soon as they came out of the womb and were cleaned up a bit, we were allowed to adjust them immediately.

SCOTT: Many people would not believe that you could or would adjust a newborn. Why is this so advantageous?

FAB: Going through the birth canal is one of the most traumatic experiences a child will ever go through because of the space involved, the pressures, and many other reasons. What we know today is that babies should be checked right after birth primarily because you want to make sure that they have not suffered any spinal misalignments caused by the twisting and turning they endure during delivery.

With Sudden Infant Death Syndrome or SIDS, babies may have had a history of a momentary lack of blood supply to the brain at birth. But when they have chiropractors checking these babies to make sure there are no problems that may cause lack of blood supply, in many cases these babies are saved. When we did *Chicken Soup for the Chiropractic Soul*®, we received many, many letters telling us of these stories.

SCOTT: What can you tell us about *Chiropractic Soul*®?

FAB: Chiropractic has had many friends over the years. Two of our good friends and big supporters for over 20 years have been Jack Canfield and Mark Victor Hansen, the co-founders of the *Chicken Soup for the Soul*® series. Together, they have sold over 100 million copies of *Chicken Soup*® books since 1993 and are continuing to grow.

We asked Jack and Mark if they would consider doing a book telling the stories of chiropractic. We felt we had the ability to get people to listen to the results by presenting them through this tremendously credible means. After we proposed the idea, both immediately said they would support the idea, because they had both personally benefited from chiropractic treatment for more than 20 years— as well as their families, staffs, friends and others they knew.

We started collecting stories over a three-month period and received over 6,000 stories or testimonials. Basically, it was one miracle after another, very compelling! We released *Chicken Soup for the Chiropractic Soul*® in June and are already on our second printing as the first printing sold out quickly. We've been fielding calls about taking the book to some of the talk shows as their producers read how compelling and life-changing these stories really are.

SCOTT: Do you see any great changes in the way patients are evaluated when they first come in versus 20 years ago?

FAB: Yes. Today, your chiropractor is more of a wellness coach, your guide, somebody who really wants to help you. In the initial assessment, we're seeing more chiropractors doing more than just the orthopedic and physical exams. They are using technology like thermograms and posture analysis, and they consider factors like dietary habits, exercise, social behaviors like alcohol consumption, smoking, how much coffee the person drinks and so on. Some even do physiological profiles.

Chiropractic is exploring far more scenarios than we looked at 20 years ago. Twenty years ago people went to the chiropractor because their neck hurt. Today, the profession is moving away from an "acute triage only" type practice. We are moving more toward a proactive evaluation that begins from childhood, to the behaviors of the family and the behaviors of the individual.

Are they standing too much, are they sitting too much, are they spending too much time on airplanes, are they sleeping enough? What are they sleeping on? What is their emotional state? Where is their stress coming from? Are they having financial issues? Are they having relationship issues? Patients come and communicate with chiropractors on a whole new level to see where chiropractic can be a resource for them.

SCOTT: As today's chiropractor becomes the "go-to" wellness provider, you have expanded the teaching at Parker to include these broader skill sets. How has that come about?

FAB: When I took this position in early 1999, I did a survey of over 4,000 alumni and asked, "Where did you feel this institution did not provide you the proper foundation for your success? Where are you finding inadequacies when a patient brings you something that you are not prepared to handle as well as it should have been"?

We took their responses to our faculty and curriculum coordinators to help in creating a curriculum that addressed the issues we uncovered, and ensured that we are able to provide the best foundation possible for future graduates. We want them to be the most trained and qualified chiropractors they can be upon graduation. Our desire is to ensure that they are the wellness doctors of the future.

SCOTT: You are one of the youngest college presidents in the nation. Where do you see your role in ten years from now?

FAB: When I was asked to take this role at 33, it was a little shocking. I didn't have 30 years of background in education. Typically, someone in my position is 50 to 75 years old. But at the same time, I have enough love and passion for this profession that I said, "If I can just listen and find out where the areas of weakness are, we can create a team that can work together to produce the best chiropractors possible." Immediately, I started weekly meetings with all key departments, which ultimately became a self-study.

Two years later the accreditation board came in to evaluate the effectiveness of our teaching. Typically, accreditation has about 457 "must statements," meaning there are 457 things you have to do in their eyes to do the best job possible to teach students. After a two-week period including interviewing students, alumni, the board, the faculty, and the staff, and sitting in class and experiencing the way Parker teaches, they gave us a perfect score, zero concerns. Everything was perfect! We were shocked!

SCOTT: A perfect score? That's amazing!

FAB: On top of that, they gave us three commendations on how high-tech we are. All of our rooms are connected to the Internet and our Intranet. Our professors use PowerPoint presentations, and we have notes and literature in our database for review. A second commendation was given for our faculty, for how outstanding they are at going above and beyond the call and really caring for their students. They also gave Parker a commendation for our own self-evaluation over the previous two years.

I see my role over the next ten years as helping to improve the education system in this country, to bring passion again to students who want to learn and most important, show them how they can apply that learning, regardless of the discipline, to better society.

SCOTT: What legacy do you want to leave behind?

FAB: My goal is to fulfill my present day to the fullest. I wake up every morning anticipating a wonderful day, and go to sleep counting my blessings for everything, and for all the things that happened in the day. If I were to predict my legacy, it would be that I have been able to communicate not just through words but through actions.

I truly believe actions speak much louder than words. The legacy will be that there are no limitations except the ones we set ourselves. It's not so much about getting there. In fact, I hope I never get there. I never want to stop being challenged. I'm truly enjoying the learning, and I'm showing that you are never too young to affect the lives of millions of people. All of us have the potential of affecting more people than we imagine, all for the better. It's only a matter of doing it.

So many people think they can only affect the lives of their close family and friends. Some people believe they can affect the lives of their customers or patients, etc. But when you begin to have a worldwide vision, everything we do within ourselves has the ability to affect the rest of the world collectively for the better. I just hope that my little contributions over the last four and a half years—and what is to come—can help make this a better world.

- To help support Parker College of Chiropractic, obtain information and make donations, go to www.parkercc.edu, or call 972-438-6932.
- To learn more about Fab, go to www.parkerseminars.com.

Dr. Dõv Baron
Surgery for the Soul

It could be said that the worst tragedy to befall Dõv Baron was also the best thing that ever happened to him. A catastrophic accident led him to re-imagine his life and find a new calling—a "soul surgeon" who helps others find true spiritual health.

SCOTT: "You're the soul surgeon." Can you tell us what that means?

DÕV: The title came out of my realization that most people are sticking band-aids over big problems and not really dealing with what needs to be dealt with. You can deal with the thoughts in your head by replacing them with positive thinking. But that's only a very small band-aid over the massive programming and conditioning that's running underneath. That conditioning is what a soul surgeon gets to. It's getting to the deep unconscious conditioning, and surgically removing it with precise technique and technology. One of my goals in life is to help people become the very best they can be, by allowing them to remove things, rather than add. Many programs fill you up with more stuff. Mine will certainly give you more tools and skills, but a big part of it is removing what's in the way.

SCOTT: One of the first evenings we were together, you were reaching out to perform that kind of surgery very quickly!

DÕV: I can't resist helping somebody who really wants to go there. I'm not interested at all in helping somebody who doesn't want to go there. There are a lot of people who feel like it's a job to help people get healthy. And even in my private practice, if somebody wants to work with me, and they're not ready to do that work, I won't do it. However, if somebody steps up and shows me that they're really keen, then we're going there, but it's not what they expect. It's much deeper. This is not superficial stuff. That's why it's soul surgery.

SCOTT: I understand that you were greatly influenced in the early stages by Dr. Martin Luther King. Can you tell us a little bit about that?

DÕV: Absolutely! Dr. Martin Luther King, Jr. was my first hero! I walked into the living room of my home, and my mother was looking at the television, crying. I had never heard of Dr. King. I was about 10 years old. I said, "Why are you crying?" And she said, "A great man is dead!" I looked at the screen and saw an image of this black man saying, "I have a dream." I felt overwhelmed with emotion listening to his speech. I asked my mom who he was, and what he did, and she told me all about the civil rights movement, and how powerful he was. There was a knowing inside of me, something that said I have to make that kind of difference. So Dr. King was my original inspiration to become a speaker regarding preventive health, someone who makes a difference for bigger masses.

SCOTT: At that point you went to work on personal development and then taking that to the masses. How did you gain that knowledge? Where did you go to seek to become that difference maker?

DÕV: My journey into personal development started as a very small child, with some particularly strange spiritual experiences that confused me and everybody around me. So at a very early age I was sent to study with some rabbis who helped me understand some of what was going on. That unconsciously pushed me into further understanding. I spent the next 20 years of my life traveling the world and studying with different spiritual masters from the East and the West, everyone from Orthodox bishops to rabbis, to teachers of Vedanta (a school of philosophy within Hinduism), Hindu wisdom, Buddhism, and many different faces from many different religions.

That was where the journey began. That actually led me, strangely enough, into psychology. I understood the metaphysical philosophies, and the separation between religion and spirituality, and a great range, a great variety of different philosophies. Yet I kept meeting people who had all these spiritual answers and whose lives were not together. They couldn't get it together to order a pizza or go to the washroom. So then I began to study psychology, and I started to find the answers to why people weren't using their spirituality more pragmatically.

Then came the next step on that path, which was almost 20 years ago. I became frustrated with myself, asking, "How come I know what to do, and I'm still making the same mistakes?" That became a really daunting question for me, drove me a little crazy for a long time, and led me to discover a book on quantum physics. That showed me how we create our reality. I began to understand that it is not a conscious process by which we create our reality, but an unconscious process. It's the things that are going on in our unconscious mind that actually manifest our reality.

Finally, I had a connection between quantum physics, metaphysics, and psychology. And I trademarked the term "quantum-meta psychology"™, which is this blend of quantum physics, metaphysics, and psychology that helps us understand how spiritual laws are identical to quantum physical laws. So the unconscious mind shows up in our everyday life, actually manifesting everything around us. That's pretty hard for most people to believe. But when you really understand it, it's actually mind-blowing. People say, "Oh my God, I have created everything around me"!

SCOTT: I want to know how you began examining fields further. But prior to that, unfortunately, you had a, shall we say, life-shattering event.

DÕV: That would be a nice understatement!

SCOTT: Or should we call it a face-shattering event?

DÕV: Yeah, maybe we should call it a face-shattering event or a crash diet—anything you like, really.

SCOTT: I understand that as you were rock climbing, you reached for a rock, it came loose, and you fell 120 feet at an estimated 70 miles an hour.

DÕV: You know, what you just said there, Scott, is interesting. It was June, 1990. I reached for a rock, and the rock dislodged a bigger rock that hit me in the face. I crashed to the ground 120 feet below. You said "unfortunately." I happily disagree with you. There was nothing unfortunate about it. It was the greatest blessing of my life. It was the thing that changed my life.

I believe that human beings have a soul that guides us. And I believe that the soul whispers, while the ego screams. The soul whispers to you, and if you don't listen then it has to turn up the volume a little bit, and then a little bit more, and then a little bit more. And if you're really dumb and deaf, like me, it turns it up so loud that you have to fall off a mountain to pay attention.

That fall was a great gift. I didn't see it that way at the time, but a couple of years after the fall, I saw that it was an incredible blessing. It woke me up, made me pay attention. I fell 120 feet, from a self-imposed pedestal, and landed on my ego. People often ask me, "You were a speaker before you fell; you worked privately with people before you fell, and so what's the difference?" The difference is, I stopped rescuing people. I stopped helping people who didn't want to be helped. I started to rescue myself. There are people in this life who will tell you up and down, "Please help me! Please help me!" But they don't really want to be helped. That was a big lesson for me. I took care of myself so I could help people who really wanted to be helped.

SCOTT: After your fall, you dealt with weight loss, shattered bones, and reconstruction, things most people would consider to be devastating. How do you take those things and turn that energy into the desire to make a difference in people's lives?

DÕV: It certainly isn't instantaneous. I had seven facial reconstructive surgeries. I was completely out of action for about a year and a half. I was mad at everybody, including God. I had the desire not to be accountable for my fall, to say, "It must have been God punishing me"! So for me, what it was about was really asking myself, "Why would I create this"? That was the turning point. If I create everything in my life, why would I create this horrible thing? So I could help myself. One of the great lessons in life that I had to learn was, "Don't deny somebody their pain. It may be the very last thing they need before they change"! If somebody had come along that day and said "Listen, don't fall, learn this lesson instead." I don't know that I would have learned the lesson.

SCOTT: You wouldn't have taken it seriously without the fall?

DÕV: I think humans need a serious consequence to take things seriously. If it's a crime to do something, and the punishment is a slap on the wrist, you don't mind taking a slap on the wrist. But if the punishment is 20 years in jail, you're going to be seriously thinking whether you want to do that. I needed that serious consequence. I think it's part of the human condition that most people have to wait until they're in serious pain before they can change. It's a sad thing, and it doesn't have to be true. It's part of my mission to say to people, "You don't need the fall if you can just pay attention." It took a huge fall off a mountain to wake me up. For some people it's a heart attack. For other people it's a divorce, or bankruptcy, or illness. But it ultimately comes back to accountability for creating your own life.

SCOTT: I think that's such a critical message. You don't need to wait for a disaster to deal with issues in your life!

DÕV: Well, I already hold the rock diving championship! Unless you really want to try a serious crash diet, and lose 50 pounds in three weeks, and have seven reconstructive surgeries, I can't really recommend that.

SCOTT: You're recognized as one of the world's leading authorities in the area of Quantum Resonance Fields (QRFs). First of all, fill us in on what QRFs are to begin with.

DÕV: Everybody and every situation has a QRF—a quantum resonance field. The simplest example is that when you walk into a room, you feel a "vibe." There's an energy present that either attracts or repels. That's the resonance of the room. Situations have a resonance—they feel comfortable or uncomfortable. People have a resonance also.

When you walk into a room, you see a particular person, and feel a pull toward them for no conscious reason, that's resonance. Resonance is the energy of a thing. For human beings, it's their emotional energy. We have a personal emotional resonance field, the emotional history we carry around with us. Your emotional history is held in a quantum field, and it resonates out from you. The more you heal your emotional history, the cleaner your field becomes.

SCOTT: Is that the process of acknowledging and releasing the past? Or is it deeper than that?

DÕV: That's part of it. But acknowledging the past and releasing the past is a huge leap. That's like going to kindergarten and coming out with a PhD. There is a lot between those two stages. Forgiving and releasing comes out of understanding yourself and why you have set

55

your life up the way you have. Because anything happening in your life is there for a good reason. Now, you may say I don't want this divorce, this bankruptcy, this sickness, whatever it is, but it's there because you're getting something out of it. The question is, "What are you getting out of it"? Very often, what you're getting out of it is, at a deep unconscious level, what you feel you deserve.

SCOTT: So when you're working with people, is the key addressing those issues to truly acknowledge and truly release them to start anew?

DÕV: I'm usually asking you to ask yourself certain questions. These will allow you to see what you've hidden from yourself so that you can release these things. In the QRF program, we go very, very deep. That is the "soul surgery." That's where we find the depth of what was placed in your quantum resonance field at an early age, so you can release it. Most of it may be outside of your immediate recall. Everybody on this planet has a perfect memory. But few people have perfect recall of that memory. We remember everything at an unconscious level.

    The unconscious is like the operating system for your mind. You have the system you loaded originally in your unconscious. And today you're using the latest version of Windows, but you don't take out the old programs. You have two programs interfering with each other. You've got your new program that you're putting in on a daily basis. But you've not removed the old program, and you're heading for a crash. That's the way the old programs work. Now when you first installed the old program, you needed it. But it may not be appropriate any more.

SCOTT: Is there an easy in-and-out process people could work with?

DÕV: It's the quantum resonance field program. It is the best thing I know. I've been a trained therapist for 20 years, and I've watched people go into therapy with other therapists, and be there for 10 or 15 years, and still not really get down to the bare bones of the problem. What I set out to do was to design a program that would allow somebody to take a giant quantum leap, in a reasonable length of time, so that they could get to the very depth of whatever the issue is, so they could release it. In that process, I show them how their operating program was installed, why, how to uninstall it, and what their new program is.

We set about putting in the new program and removing the old. Whether they choose to continue removing the old is their business. But this is a powerful way to get into it, and it shifts people's lives dramatically! It's absolutely demanding, but is a great alternative to 10 years of therapy. The quickest way to get results is to begin asking, "Why would I create this in my life"? If you don't believe that you created it, just say, "Well, let's pretend that I created this. Why would I want that"? This question alone will take you on a journey into your deep unconscious so you can identify your specific program, and find the truth of who you are.

SCOTT: I've learned some of the process. It really provides powerful responsibility and/or freedom.

DÕV: You just said something that's very insightful, and I want to reiterate it. You mentioned responsibility and freedom. That's the most important thing. In order to have the life of your imagining, you have to take responsibility. But taking that responsibility is the only way to freedom. The bizarre thing is we don't want freedom without responsibility. Dude, you can't get free unless you take responsibility! It's the only way. When you take full responsibility for your life, then you begin to see that you can create whatever you want. I love the words of Fredalem Wolsa, a quantum physicist: "There is no out there, out there. There's only in here, out there!" It is your consciousness that is out there. What is happening in your reality is coming from who you are in here. When you change that, you change everything!

SCOTT: I know you are successfully taking this message across many different groups in many different sectors and are seeing great individual growth. But one of the purposes of this book is certainly to bring out the philanthropic interest of the "Giants" we're talking with. I know you actively support a couple of organizations. Tell me a little bit about Triage.

DÕV: Triage is an amazing group of people! I said earlier I want to help people who want to help themselves. I don't want to help people who don't want to help themselves. Triage is amazing, because it helps people who really want to help themselves. It takes people who are on the street, who don't want to be on the street any more—those who want to be somewhere else—and gives them direct help to start cleaning up their act. It gives them clothing, food, and shelter. It gets them off the street, maybe into their first set of new clothes or decent clothes, so they can go to an interview, get a job, and make a fresh start. I'm very supportive of Triage. They take direct donations of money, and clothes, pots, and pans, and towels, sheets, and bedding–they're fabulous!

SCOTT: Where is Triage located?

DÕV: I believe there is a version of Triage in every city. I know of them in Canada, and they are the ones I work with directly. But you can certainly contact them at www.triage.ca. They do amazing work!

SCOTT: You also support anything that's in support of abused women. Can you tell us a little bit about that?

DÕV: In my first five years of being a therapist, I specialized in working with women who had been abused. I'm a very big advocate of support groups that help abused people who have been molested. Because there are so many groups involved in this, I'm not going to name off one. But I would love to see people find those groups and work for them, whether it's as volunteers or giving them support, financial or otherwise. One in four women in the United States is molested. Think about that the next time you go to a party. In a room with 100 women, 25 of those women have been molested. And that's only the women who have actually come out and said so.

There are many people in these situations who need help, and what they need most is empowerment. They need to know that they're powerful enough to walk away from these situations. The only reason any woman would stay in that situation is because she doesn't believe she's powerful enough to leave. She believes this is the only person who will love her. By showing love and compassion to these people, and helping them to help themselves, we make a difference in the world that is felt by their children, our children, and our children's children. These numbers are inexcusable. They are epidemic, and have to change!

SCOTT: I think of my 18-year-old daughter and those numbers make me cringe!

DÕV: If you ask your daughter, you'll discover she knows many girls who have been through it. We've got this idea that this is a socio-economic problem affecting only people who are in a lower financial bracket. It's not. It's happening across the board. It's happening in your neighborhood. Not just in poverty. In every neighborhood, in every gender, in every race men and women are being molested. The other ignorance is that we think it's just women. So many men have gone through this. It's enormous, scary–the numbers are so big.

SCOTT: What other thoughts would you like to leave with our readers?

DÕV: Well, really it's a reiteration. And that is the quote that I gave you earlier. In life you don't get what you deserve. You get what you believe you deserve at a deep unconscious level. No level of positive thinking is going to change that. It is only through examining yourself, and asking for the help you need, that things change. It's your reality, you're creating it, and you are free to create the life of your imagining! You have the power!

- To help support Triage, obtain information and make donations, go to www.Triage.ca, or call 604-254-3700.
- To learn more about Dõv, go to www.igniteyoursoul.com or www.baronmastryinstitute.com.

Ed Young
Fellowship Church's Dynamic Leader

As the founding and senior Pastor at Fellowship Church in Grapevine, Texas, one of the fastest growing churches in the country, Ed Young's leadership and vision are second to none. For nearly 16 years, his clarity of vision and never ending enthusiasm have lead the church that started as the Las Colinas Baptist Church with 38 people, to grow to a membership of over 20,000 people today.

SCOTT: Ed, from the beginning, you have always been willing to modify your approach as a church. Many subtle changes have taken place along the way. How have they come about?

ED: The first such change came November 6, 1991, when the church dropped Baptist from the name and became Fellowship of Las Colinas. This was a small but positive change resulting in reaching more people for Christ. People from various backgrounds responded who otherwise may not have been reached. The goal of our church was to meet people where they are, and present Jesus to them. During the first full year as a church, 563 new members were reached and added to the church family. We baptized 128 new Christians during the church's first year.

SCOTT: The Fellowship Church has always been creative in attracting people. Can you give us an idea of some of the events you developed?

ED: The events were innovative and unconventional for churches at that time. They included a baseball clinic with professional baseball players, a concert featuring Al Denson, and the annual Noah's Ark-fest (an alternative for Halloween) with children dressing as one of the animals in the ark. We brought in (motivational speaker) Zig Ziglar as a guest speaker, developed a Beach Retreat for our youth at Panama City Beach, Florida, and held an Angelic Creations Craft Fair and Style Show where people shared craft ideas.

All of these events were tremendous successes and really created the church's most effective word-of-mouth advertising around the Dallas/Ft. Worth Metroplex in the early days.

SCOTT: Starting as a mission outreach church, and not having a building, where did you meet?

ED: The church was meeting in rented facilities in MacArthur Commons Complex in Irving, Texas. When the Irving Arts Center was completed, the church negotiated a rental agreement with them to use the Arts Center for Sunday morning worship. In late 1992 and early 1993, a land team was selected and began looking for land for a church home. In June 1993 the team located a parcel of 159.4 acres of land in Grapevine, Texas. The land was owned by Resolution Trust Corporation and was offered on a closed bid basis. Fellowship Church bid $2,500,000, as did the other two land giants who were also bidding. God provided, and Fellowship Church was awarded the contract.

On July 18, 1993 we told the church we would have to pay down $625,000. The church raised this amount in four weeks. On May 10, 1994, Fellowship Church closed on the purchase of this land. The membership was approximately 2,100 at that time and the thought that we could raise the money and provide the down payment is amazing.

SCOTT: How did you continually increase your attendance?

ED: We set out to create a user-friendly environment in which people are exposed to uncompromising biblical truths. Our generation also wants to know how to live out these truths, Monday through Saturday, so we place a high premium on creativity in communicating these truths.

SCOTT: What type of creativity are you referring to?

ED: That collective creativity was highlighted in each worship service designed weekly around a particular theme that was relevant to everyday living. Some of the pertinent topics around that time included "All in the Family," "Back to the Future/Learning from the Decades," "Honesty," "Questions I've Always Wanted to Ask God," "Faces of Fear" and "Discovering My Significance." Each week's particular message in a series was and still is prefaced by music and sometimes a staged drama that interacts with the message to convey a certain biblical truth in a contemporary and relevant manner.

SCOTT: I know a lot of that happened in rented facilities. What happened once the new church was opened?

ED: We moved into our new church home on April 5, 1998 with 9,602 in attendance including all of our guests. Membership at that time was approximately 6,500. Our average weekly attendance went from almost 5,000 up to about 6,600. We started in our new church home with two identical weekend services—one on Saturday evening and one on Sunday morning.

On August 8, 1999 we added a second Sunday service and our attendance jumped to over 9,000 per weekend. By August 2001, all services were over 80 percent full again, so a second Saturday service was added. Attendance was running around 12,000 people, and after adding the fourth service, attendance jumped to over 14,000 on an average. We've continued to add services, and at the present time, attendance has climbed up to almost 20,000 at times, and membership is now 18,648 at the time of this interview.

SCOTT: How have you been able to accomplish such an amazing feat?

ED: We have continually removed the barriers that keep people from coming to church. I sum up those barriers in three categories: boring services that don't relate to life, the perception that the church is more interested in someone's money than in them, and fear of being put on the spot. The techniques are paying off. Most of our members are not from Baptist backgrounds. We have former agnostics, Buddhists, Catholics, atheists and Jews. You find a wide range of socioeconomic levels here, from CEOs of corporations to those who are looking for employment.

We present the message without compromise. What we have done is change the methodology to reach people wherever they are. We strive for excellence in all that we do. If it's worth doing, it's worth doing right. We have a tremendous opportunity, and we try to do everything in a way that acknowledges our gratitude to God for letting us serve Him here at this time. Our goal is to provide every race of people from every walk of life with a safe environment to hear a dangerous message. Each move has brought more challenges and more opportunities to reach people for Christ.

SCOTT: You have had a vivid vision to grow the Fellowship Church to the point it has reached today. Where does that vision come from?

ED: When I think about vision, my mind rushes to the book of Proverbs. Proverbs 29:18—this is a pretty cool verse. It says, "Where there is no vision, the people perish." It's pretty straightforward. So, if there is vision, people thrive. God is always working with vision. The vision of Fellowship Church unfolded in a very unique way.

SCOTT: Vision is obviously very important, but vision by itself doesn't get the job done. What was the next big factor in the explosive growth of the Fellowship?

ED: God gave us the vision, and then He added something else. He gave us leaders. Vision plus leaders equal difference makers. When the church brought me here, it was just starting. I was the only staff member. I had a rented typewriter and we were meeting in rented facilities.

A small group of people looked at me and said, "Ed, how are you going to make the church grow when you are the only staff member"? It was a great question. I said, "You know what? You're going to be my staff. That's right. You're going to be the staff of Fellowship of Las Colinas. I can't pay you. We don't have the money, but you're going to be the staff."

SCOTT: Who were those people?

ED: One was Owen Goff. I remember Owen telling me, "You know, a long time ago, I said to myself, "I will do anything it takes to reach people." Preston Mitchell was another. Preston told me, "You know, I knew there had to be something better." Of course, there was Doris Scoggins. She said, "I knew there were so many people out there that needed to be reached, but I just didn't know what was going to happen. I knew something was out there, something was happening."

SCOTT: Owen was in the insurance business, Preston was in the utilities business, and Doris was also in the private sector. They are a pretty diverse group to say the least. What happened next?

ED: I gathered them together and said, "We're going to make some decisions here. We need to commit not to miss a Sunday (because at that time we only had church on Sunday). We need to commit to attend every Sunday morning for the next eighteen months. We've got to get this thing off the ground. We've got to become autonomous and self-supporting. We've got to do it. I'm willing to do it, are you"? And they responded, "Yes."

Is that amazing? You are talking about awesome leaders! The commitment level was huge. They put flesh beneath the vision. It's so important to understand that principle, because every time God adds a vision, he adds it to the lives of leaders. He always adds leaders to carry the vision through. So many churches are set up to fail. Their leadership structure is not biblical.

SCOTT: What do you mean?

ED: Let me use an example of a dentist's office. Let's say a dentist has been in his practice for four years. Then let's say that fifteen of his patients decide they are going to form a committee. The dentist can't make any decisions without them voting on it, and it has to be unanimous. Do you think the dentist would stay in business long? Of course not!

That's the way most churches have been set up. The pastor gets a great staff and there's this board of fifteen people who don't know up from down about the church. Yet, they are going to tell the leaders how to lead. That's not a biblical model of church.

Here is where most churches mess up. A pastor, a staff member, or a leader has a "vertical" vision from God. Boom! God gives it to them. They begin to do the "horizontal" stuff God calls for, things begin to grow, things begin to happen, and they begin to create.

Suddenly, though, there's one or two negative people who rear their ugly heads and say, "Well, the music's too loud," or, "I don't like the way you said that," or, "The service...," or, "The parking...," or, "I didn't like...blah, blah, blah." And then the pastor goes, "Oh." Then someone with a lot of money says, "You know, if we continue down this road, I'm just going to leave." The pastor says, "Oh. He can't leave! He's Mr. Big Time! Oh! We'll change and we'll appease you, Mr. Big Time. Listen, we'll do what you want us to do."

SCOTT: So you're saying too many cooks?

ED: If the leadership incorporates too many things outside the vision, things get messed up. The church starts saying, "It's just about us four and no more, the holy huddle. Let's look at the lint in other Christians' navels." And they flip off their community and say, "Go to hell! Our church is for the white hats. The sinners, you're the black hats, and you can't show up here. It's just about our little deal, our little clique, our little country club, our little words, our little world." They end up talking "Christianese."

SCOTT: It's obvious that you believe strongly in the vertical vision with horizontal execution. What else does it take to have a church grow?

ED: You've got vision plus leaders and then add something else, commitment. You can talk about leaders, and you can talk about vision—those things are good. Leaders carry out the vision. They are intertwined like peanut butter and jelly, or chips and hot sauce. But you've also got to talk about commitment, because it takes a commitment by the leaders to the vision. It's the commitment to reach up, reach out, and reach in, which really puts wheels beneath what God is doing when He wants to add and do something awesome like He has done, and is doing, and will do at Fellowship Church.

I was really ignorant as a senior pastor. Recently we had several pastors from Florida shadow us in a leadership-training exercise. One of the pastors, Ron, specializes in training pastors on how to start churches, and we were talking about Fellowship Church. He said, "Ed, I don't know if you know this or not, but 80 percent of churches that start up fail in the first year. They have to close the doors."

Eighty percent! That's a lot! Think about how a church is started and after twelve months—boom! Then he continued, "And Ed, I'll tell you something else. When I talk to all these pastors starting churches, if the church makes it past twelve months, most of the people will leave the church after eighteen months."

"Now," I said, "I understand it. Now, I get it."

SCOTT: What was the revelation?

ED: Our church started, and we had this vision—reach up, reach out, reach in. Great things were taking place. But after about eighteen months, I noticed that most of the people who started with us were bolting, leaving. Even some of the people on the pastor's search team that brought me here and said, "Ed, I'll be with you, man. I'm here with the vision. I own it! It's mine." Even some of them said, "See ya."

I came home one night and I said, "Lisa, I didn't sign up for this. Man, I'm out of here. I'm gone. I didn't plan on having to bust my rear to lead this church, and preach, and all the stuff I have to do just for people to leave. No wonder Dallas/Ft. Worth is the way it is with all these mean Christians."

Christians are the only ones who shoot the wounded. We say, "Oh, you're a Christian and you messed up! You're out of here! We'll show him." But I didn't leave. I came very close. I've never told the church that before. I was *that* close, but I didn't. Do you know why? Commitment!

SCOTT: What does commitment mean to you?

ED: It means to pledge yourself to a position no matter what the cost. When I was praying about leading this church and becoming pastor, I said, "God, I'm here. I'm committed to what you're going to do, and I don't care what happens. God, I'm going to stay here. I'm committed to it." And that is what held me here. I didn't feel like it. The polls didn't say, "Hey, you know, you should stay." And the same is true for the other leaders.

SCOTT: What happened as a result of everyone's commitment?

ED: God was replacing the people who left ten to one while this was happening. Isn't that amazing? We didn't have any bloodshed or fights in the church. These people just left to attend other churches that suited them better. But commitment is what it's all about. We're committed to the vision. Had Preston and Owen and Doris and I gone somewhere else and started some other church, and just said, "Hey, you know, it's just too tough," we would have missed one of the greatest rides that God has ever given the local church in Christian history.

Our staff will take on hell with a Super Soaker®. That's how committed we are to the vision. It's totally a God thing—totally. It is amazing what God has done through commitment. The commitment level of our church blows me away. And it blows many other Christian leaders away around the country.

SCOTT: Are you referring to the Creative Church Conference (C3) held at the Fellowship each January?

ED: Yes, it's phenomenal! The C3 conference encourages church organizations to increase creativity in just about everything that they do in church. We teach people not just to be disciples, but also to grow disciples. It also helps church staffs break through the boredom barrier by showing them how to creatively work together as a team. It's a very exciting three days.

People go to church and too often think, "Wow, this is wearing me out!" Too much same old, irrelevant stuff—the aqueduct system in ancient Samaria, and Solomon's forty thousand horse stables, and what types of horses he owned. What is up with that? People need help. They're drowning in their marriage or maybe their career. They're drowning and are in need of being rescued. That's why people need creativity in the church. Church should be the most creative thing around.

A great commitment to the Great Commandment and the Great Commission demands great creativity. A great commitment, pledging yourself to a position no matter what the cost, to the Great Commandment, loving God with all your heart, soul, mind and body, loving your neighbor as yourself, and the Great Commission, go and make disciples, baptize—it all demands great creativity. If you ever go to a church and you are bored, don't blame God. Blame the communicators, singers, and leaders. Blame the people who are leading the church.

SCOTT: Can you tell us what has happened in the last year?

ED: I look back over the last twelve months and I realize that we baptized 2,262 new believers. I think about our small group ministry. We have over 230 home-team groups with 4,300 plus adults in small group Bible study. Several weekends ago, we had 19,561 people walk through the doors of Fellowship Church. I think about the fact that on an average weekend, we'll have nearly 5,000 children here at Fellowship Church.

I think about our Web site. It has ten million hits a month. I think about our television show that's going around the world. I think about our nationally syndicated radio show. I think about the church we just started in Mostreal, Brazil, where Owen and a group of people are helping in that effort. I think about all the parking staff who brave the elements outside our building each weekend. I think about our ushers and I think about our extravagant hospitality folks. I think about our children's workers and youth workers, and those who work in athletics.

SCOTT: You mentioned having more than 5,000 children over the weekend services. How do you teach so many young children?

ED: We have a church that believes in teaching our children age-appropriate Bible studies. Each weekend a child can be part of an exciting and active environment filled with songs, games, and loveable characters that teach Godly values. Our children's services meet at the same time as adult services. The children are experiencing the creative, life-changing worship of Fellowship Church, just as their parents did.

SCOTT: Is what you have been able to accomplish simply executing Jesus' model of teaching?

ED: Exactly! If you're talking about innovation and creativity, all you have to do is think about Jesus. He never used the same method. He always was changing, drawing in the sand, pointing to a flower, He was picking up a child, He was talking about a building that was falling down, and He was using the street vernacular of the day. He was the master teacher, the master communicator. Over 70 percent of his words were words of relevancy and application. That's a pretty good model.

Simple things like a block or a ball aren't going to break. We have a very simple structure here and we want to do things so that people understand them. The greatest compliment you can give Fellowship Church is to say this, "That was simple."

- To help support Fellowship Church, obtain information and make donations, go to www.fellowshipchurch.com, or call 972-471-5700. You can drop by and visit at 2450 Highway 121 North, Grapevine, Texas 76051.
- To learn more about Ed, go to www.EdYoung.com.

70

Orrin Hudson
Checkmating Life

Orrin Hudson's story is a classic Horatio Alger-style American success story. Born one of a huge family in the South, poor and living in public housing, he made himself into an exceptional scholar. He began a career in law enforcement and finally moved on to his proudest venture: BeSomeone, a non-profit organization that helps children build bright futures by helping them learn life skills through chess.

SCOTT: Orrin, please tell us a little bit about where you were raised.

ORRIN: I was brought up in Birmingham, Alabama. I had six brothers and six sisters—six older than I, and six younger. I was definitely in the middle. I learned early in life that you become what you think about, and that has nothing to do with your circumstances. You can overcome your circumstances if you're willing to get near the right people, learn from the experts, and try to be the best you can be.

SCOTT: I understand that you were voted the most likely to succeed in your senior year in high school.

ORRIN: Yes. I always worked while attending school. In high school, I sold shoes and, of course, made a lot of money, and it kind of helped me.

SCOTT: How did you make the move to become an Alabama State Trooper?

ORRIN: You know, I've always been committed to serving others, helping, and protecting others. That's been my motto in life—always give more than you receive. I just thought I could make a difference in the community by doing it. So I applied, and I took the test. They gave six hundred people the test, and they were only going to hire one hundred. I was number thirty-three, so I got in. It was an opportunity to really make a difference and an impact, and I learned a lot in the meantime.

SCOTT: I know after that, you became an entrepreneur and opened some businesses. What made you make that change?

ORRIN: Well, all my life, and especially as a shoe salesman, I had been trained that the customer is always right. But when I became a State Trooper, the formula changed. It turned into, "The customer is always wrong!" So I've always kept both approaches: the entrepreneurial spirit of treating the customer with respect and always doing the right thing, and also, being a bit of a Trooper, being tough and no-nonsense. Sometimes, I'm too nice of a guy. For example, I can remember a time when I was a Trooper and we had to close the road. Well, let's say you have a family but you can't get home without going through the police barricade. And if you don't have a license, you're afraid to come through at all. The area I worked was a poor area, and a lot of the people in the area didn't have licenses. If I write you a ticket for that, it is going to cost you about $500. I can't write a ticket like that—it hurts me. That's too much money out of someone's pocket. I just care so much about people. So I came to the point where I got more into the entrepreneurial side of things.

SCOTT: How did you make the move into personal development?

ORRIN: I've always been into personal development. I've got a whole system. I listened to some of Tony Robbins training, and it turned my life around! I just started growing and learning from other people. I learned about Jim Rohn, Tony Robbins, and Jack Canfield, people who inspired me to reach for the top.

SCOTT: How did you develop your interest in chess?

ORRIN: When I was fourteen years old, my brother showed me how to play. Later, my high school teacher, James Ed, took my game to another level. He coached me and mentored me for four years. And when I graduated from high school, he bought me a chess book. I tore up that book going through it so much. The pages were all destroyed. It helped me build a foundation. Chess offers so many life lessons. You have to concentrate, focus—wherever you are, be there. You have to be there in order to be on top!

SCOTT: How did you develop your game to become a champion?

ORRIN: I developed my game by getting around the right people, playing stronger people, learning from the experts, reading, and through practice, practice, and practice. Practice makes perfect! You have to make sure you are practicing things that are solid. For example, I was teaching this player some time ago. He suddenly said, "Orrin, that's wrong"!

I asked him, "Why?"

"I've always been taught this way," he replied.

I said, "Let's play a game, and I'll show you why that's not wrong"!

So I played him, and I beat him.

His response was, "Wow! How did you know"?

"Because you've been practicing wrong"!

SCOTT: One point for the teacher!

ORRIN: You've got to make sure that you're practicing with the right information, even if you're ready to learn from your mistakes. Ask yourself if what you're doing can lead you to where you want to go.

SCOTT: You told me a story about entering a City Chess Championship, thinking you had very little chance of performing well, and ended up winning it.

ORRIN: My coach told me if I got a draw, it would be a miracle. But I ended up winning the whole tournament. I had the vision. I saw myself winning the trophy. That's why visualization is so important. I went in there and told the director I was going to win. He told me I was crazy, because they had the current State champion there, the three-time amateurs' champion, and many very skilled college professors. But I was able to win it because I saw myself winning the trophy. When asked, God will come to the rescue, because let me tell you, I was not the best player there, but I got it done.

SCOTT: What kind of guidance did you receive?

ORRIN: I beat this Russian international master, Rachis Ziganov, in another tournament. He said something to me that blew my mind, "Orrin, the only reason you beat me was you were getting help from God"! And he's right! When I was playing him, the pieces were moving by themselves.

SCOTT: That's awesome!

ORRIN: I thank God for my life! It's amazing how the universe will come to your aid when you're trying to help others!

SCOTT: How did "BeSomeone.org" and "Be Someone, Inc." all come about?

ORRIN: I saw on the news that seven people were shot in the head, execution style, for $2,000. It took my breath away! That was something only someone in utter desperation would do, restrain seven people with duct tape, march them into a cooler, and shoot them in the head. That was this man's reality! I said, I'm going to start a program in which I can do something before young people go wrong. I wanted to prevent things, to show people some moves before they got on a chessboard, to practice ahead of time, to study defense. That's why professional players study defense and patterns. Chess teaches pattern recognition. Pattern recognition is the key to success in all fields. The more patterns you can recognize, the smarter and more successful you are. You can sometimes predict the future based on patterns. That's what Bill Gates is able to do. Now he's one of the richest men in the world.

SCOTT: How do you use chess to teach youth life skills?

ORRIN: Number one is pattern recognition. Number two is, the only thing that can take you to your goals is your mind. So you have to be willing to use your mind, and follow through on good ideas. Most people don't follow through. They have great ideas, but they never do anything about them. Successful people are successful because they make a habit of doing what unsuccessful people don't do—bring their ideas into reality, to completion. So we get kids in the habit of taking action, following through using all of their resources.

I use chess because it teaches responsibility. If you lose a game in chess, you have only yourself to blame. Your game will only get better when you get better. I teach it because it promotes will power. I was playing a guy the other day, and I lost my queen and both my rooks. And

I told him, "I like my position"! He told me I was crazy, but I ended up checkmating him. Why? He got materialistic—looking only at what he could gain, but not understanding the whole pattern. In fact, I was playing Jack Canfield the other day in chess. He took my rook and a bishop. So he was winning, right? No! I ended up checkmating him. Why? He got greedy—trying to take too much, too fast. Greed will get you every time.

SCOTT: What other lessons does the game teach?

ORRIN: Man, there are so many. For example, the king is the weakest piece on the chessboard. But the king is smart. He knows he's the weakest piece, so he surrounds himself with pieces that can make moves he cannot. He has a queen, which is the most powerful piece on the board, and he situates himself next to his queen. That's the key to success—attitude, association, and action. Oh, I just came up with that! You've got to have a positive attitude. You've got to associate with positive people. And you've got to take action!

SCOTT: How do the kids you work with accept this approach? Are they all open to it from the beginning?

ORRIN: They love it, because I make learning fun. This person came up to me, and said, "Orrin, the kids don't want to leave your program, but they don't realize what they're learning"! They think it's just a game. But I'm teaching them valuable life lessons they can use over and over again.

SCOTT: Tell me one of your stories about disarming some youths, getting guns out of their hands, and trading them for chessboards.

ORRIN: A television show brought me around to a housing project for about three months. I interviewed this lady who used to call her child, "the child from hell" because he was carrying guns, and hanging around with people with guns, and doing drugs, you name it. But I told him, "The key to success is not about money, is not about bling-bling, is not about a car, and a house. The key to success is making a difference while you're here. So here's what I want you to do: I want you to focus on how you can help other people. How you can add value to them. You can never take more than you give. When you give, it comes back." I taught him to be focused on how he can give. I told him that's what true success is. Look at Oprah Winfrey. She's mega-rich because she serves people. The more people you serve, and serve well, the more money you make.

I can tell you stories that will make you cry. For example, this white lady was in this high-crime area, and she was about to catch a bus. She was real scared, because she knew she was in an all-black neighborhood, and she was white. She saw this big, tall black guy approaching her across the street. She remembered what she'd learned in my class. I taught her that everybody wants to be of value. They want to serve. So she said to this big, black guy, "Will you stand here next to me until my bus comes"? And he did. When the bus came and she was getting on, she noticed that he was crying. She asked him why, and he said, "Because I was gonna rape you! But you made me feel important, you asked me help to you"!

SCOTT: Wow that sends a chill!

ORRIN: Yeah!

SCOTT: What's your biggest challenge right now?

ORRIN: Keeping the program alive. Right now, I'm about to lose my program. It's that tight. But I know I'm doing God's work, and God's going to make a way. I need all the help I can get with the program, because the program is in financial trouble.

SCOTT: That's one of the reasons this book is being written. What you're doing in Atlanta and around the country is far too valuable—it needs to grow! You're giving inner city youth the means to truly change their lives. Their changes will impact others positively!

ORRIN: Thank you.

SCOTT: Tell me a little bit about the "Win By Choice" program.

ORRIN: As you know, life is full of choices. The choices you make will determine your destiny. We all have the same resources. When you're playing a game of chess, I have sixteen pieces, and you have sixteen. It is the quality of your choices that will determine your success. It's how you use your resources. You have everything you need to succeed. You just have to figure out how to use it. And when you focus on how you can help others, that's how you get the greatest success. "Win By Choice" is about showing children and adults that you can achieve whatever you want if you focus on how you can help and add value to others. Don't just satisfy the customer. Delight the customer!

SCOTT: How can the readers of *Talking With Giants!*™ help?

ORRIN: Make a donation. Support our cause, provide guidance, and provide resources. Refer other people to make a donation. Truly, our program is in trouble. I'm on the right road, because I can tell from the feedback. But at the same time, most people are assuming my program is fully funded. It's not. They say, "You're in the USA today. It's got to be funded." It's not. They see that we've got it going on. But we need help!

SCOTT: So financial donation is one possibility. How about events, sponsorships, or things like that?

ORRIN: Yeah, exactly! Sponsor our cause. We're looking for a building right now, so we can really do some training. Right now we're bouncing around in community centers, churches, and schools. But we need something of our own. I'm constantly expanding what I know, and am constantly trying to improve the program. I'm continually finding ways to help more people be productive. Because here's the deal: a child is always going astray. If we don't help him, he's going to rob me, and you. You can make one wrong move in life and never recover.

SCOTT: I've just come to know you as somebody who really does care and wants to make a difference.

ORRIN: Everyone you meet can teach you something. That's why I have a formula that says, "For everyone you meet, treat them better than you want to be treated." That's a Double Platinum Orrin Hudson Rule. If you have that attitude, you'll never go wrong!

SCOTT: So you go beyond the Golden Rule?

ORRIN: Yeah! It's the difference between sympathy and empathy. Sympathy is saying, "I feel sorry for you." But empathy is different. That's saying, "I understand you." Empathy is when you see a guy who's going to jump off a building, and you say, "Mr. Jones, I see you're going to jump off that building. I'll jump with you"! That's empathy! You've got to put yourself in that person's shoes.

SCOTT: Do you have anything that we haven't covered?

ORRIN: "BeSomeone" is about helping others. It is about making the world better. So many need our help. Together we can make a difference!

SCOTT: Thank you for your efforts on behalf our today's disadvantaged youth!

- To help Orrin, contact him at www.BeSomeone.org. You can buy his latest book, *One Move at a Time*, buy extra books as gifts for others to pay it forward, hire Orrin to speak to your organization, or simply donate to BeSomeone to further its' reach.
- To help support "BeSomeone," obtain information, and make donations, please contact http://www.BeSomeone.org or call 678-526-0292.

T. Harv Eker
Reaching Your Peak Potential

How do you go from broke to being a millionaire in just two and a half years? If you're T. Harv Eker, you do it by following the same principles you teach to others today through your Peak Performance Institute seminars. Author of the bestselling Speed Wealth and one of the most sought-after success and wealth building speakers in the nation, Harv shares with us his secrets for success through taking action.

SCOTT: Harv, your seminar style is so alive, and so effective. How did you come about that?

HARV: It's called accelerated training. It's built around technology that helps you learn faster, remember more, and have a lot more fun while you're learning. It's based on the frame that what you hear, you tend to forget, and what you see, you tend to remember, but what you do, you understand. So there's a lot of doing things, a lot of experiential aspects to the program. It's a high-intensity experiential event. People tend to remember it for the rest of their lives, and once they remember it, they actually go ahead and do it.

SCOTT: You started out by saying we don't have to believe a word you are saying. That you are simply going to relate to your experiences. Why did you set the stage that way?

HARV: The main reason is to disarm people's skepticism from a training standpoint. When people think you're there to shove something down their throats, they're not going to listen. Or they're going to be listening in a negative manner. That's one reason I talk to them like that. But the other reason is that's what I believe. I believe you don't have to take everything as gospel. There are way too many people out there providing information about success who've never been there. They've never created success themselves. They come from a life of books and tapes. They can certainly help people, but there's no reason to take what they say as gospel. I say think for yourself. If it doesn't make sense to you, drop it. But before you do, recognize that my success in this area has been greater than yours, so maybe I know what I'm talking about.

SCOTT: I'm intrigued by your comment "How you do anything is how you do everything"! Can you expand on that?

HARV: Well, you know there are no isolated incidents. A lot of people say that they're one way, but their actions show something else. Someone might say, "I'm a very participatory person. I'm very open, I'm very understanding, I'm very positive"! But then you see them in front of you, and they're just sitting there, arms crossed, they won't stand up, they won't get involved. Their action shows that they're not open. Put the heat on any person, and you'll see what they're really like. Talk is cheap.

SCOTT: You said that two people sitting next to each other can have and share the exact same experience, and end with a different result. What makes that difference?

HARV: The difference is their thinking pattern, their way of perceiving things, and primarily their blueprints for success or non-success. Most people have a blueprint for non-success based on their past programming.

SCOTT: One of the concepts that hit home with me was saying that I had to reset my financial thermostat. Can you expand on that?

HARV: The financial thermostat is your financial blueprint. A good example would be Donald Trump. Here's a multi-billionaire who's obviously very successful. His way of thinking, the files in his mind and his decision making, all create success. When he has an opportunity, he takes advantage of it and creates success with it. Most people have the same opportunity, but they won't create success with it. Why? Because they don't think the same way that Donald Trump does. The way we think determines our actions.

SCOTT: Right.

HARV: The mind is nothing more than a big file cabinet that stores information. So why do you think differently than the person next to you, and down the hall, and down the street? It's because the files in your mind are different from theirs. So the question then becomes, how did you get those files? It's your programming, your conditioning process, your domestication, the way you grew up, and what you heard about, what you saw, what you modeled out of incidents. You formulated these files, and now you live your life based on them. Right and wrong, good and bad, true and false, your actions are all based on these files.

SCOTT: So there is a combination of all the verbal programming, modeling and specific incidents that have happened throughout your life?

HARV: Yes. A lot of it happens when you're young, because that's when you're most vulnerable. You keep replicating that same situation over and over again.

SCOTT: After listening to you, I identified my personal limiting belief regarding income. I went to a specific event that happened thirty-one years ago that I thought was long forgotten. I was amazed at how that programming stuck with me.

HARV: In the Millionaire Mind Intensive, this is where we actually do the work—we actually change people's blueprints that weekend. We don't let them walk out with their old blueprint. We actually do the work, where you go into your past situation, and you really look at what you learned about money and success, what you saw, and what experiences you got involved in. People end up a little in shock. We call those things weeds. All it takes is one major weed to transform what you think about money or success. Here's an example: a woman we had who, when she was a girl, her parents gave her a dollar to buy lunch at school. Every day, she met up with this bully who beat her up and took her money. She didn't want to be embarrassed, so she wouldn't tell anybody about it. Probably she was pleading with her mom: "Mom, don't give me a quarter! I don't want any more money. I'll make my own way for lunch!" She figured if she didn't have it, she wouldn't get beat up for it. Does that make sense?

SCOTT: Yeah, absolutely.

HARV: So today this person's, her files tell her that if she has money, she's going to get pain. And if she doesn't have money, everything will be okay. That's her subconscious conditioning process. Does it make sense? No. But does it make sense in her subconscious files? Perfect sense!

SCOTT: That's unfortunate.

HARV: She hasn't got a clue why she sabotages herself. And it's all in order to make certain that she doesn't have any money, because money causes pain. All you can do is make decisions based on the files that are in your head. What we do is change those files, so that you just make your normal, natural decisions.

SCOTT: You said that there are two types of people: successes and victims, and those victims leave three indelible clues. What are they?

HARV: The first clue is blame. They blame other people, they blame everything in their lives, on someone or something else—they blame the government, they blame their industry, their job, their business, everything. But most people don't realize that they're blaming. People who are blamers are victims, because the power is outside of them. That makes them a victim automatically.
The second clue is justification, where they justify their situation by making up something that sounds, again, perfectly normal to them. The example I use a lot is when people say: "Well, money is not that important"! Now, if they said their husband, wife, boyfriend, or girlfriend weren't that important, they won't be around for a day longer. They don't recognize it that this is a justification. Well, let me tell you something: you're not going to find any rich people who say money is not important.

SCOTT: Makes sense.

HARV: The mind is good at protecting itself. The third clue is complaining. Complaining is the worst thing you can do to your health or wealth, because it's so negative and accomplishes nothing. When you are complaining, it's not because things are going well. So you focus attention on what's not going well in your life, and you attract more of it. You become a crap magnet, and you don't even realize it.

SCOTT: That ties into your conviction that we create everything in our life, and everything not in our life. You express the belief that change has to happen at a cellular level. What does that mean?

HARV: If you change the inner programming and the physical programming, then you have a chance for a real change. But if you only do it on a mental basis, it'll be much more difficult. So the idea of having a cellular change is that we actually have to change the inner blueprint. We change people's mind files, but we also change you on a physical basis. The mind is not only in the brain. The mind is in every cell of your body. We need to change the cellular structure, so that the information that the cells are passing along to the next set of cells is different than it was the first time. Is that making any sense?

SCOTT: Absolutely!

HARV: Billions of cells die every second and billions of cells are growing. Information is passed along between them that determine how they behave. Our program impacts people at that cellular level. By the end, people are finding that they think different—they're laughing at how they used to think three days ago. They can't believe what they wrote down, what they thought about money and success. They don't buy it any more. It's ridiculous to them. So we've changed them on a cellular level.

SCOTT: Is it about changing their awareness?

HARV: No. When we do a talk, it's about awareness. But when we do the actual program it's much deeper. We do very specific, high-impact technologies, exercises and processes that make the changes right then and there. The first thing is awareness, and the second step is understanding–knowing where the programming came from, so you can disassociate yourself from it.

SCOTT: I see.

HARV: For example, a lot of people say that rich people are greedy. But are they? So we go back, and we find out the person heard that from his grandmother. She kept on saying it. But the person took it as a validation that rich people are greedy. So now he runs his life based on that. If he believes that rich people are greedy, bad people, and he doesn't want to be a greedy, bad person, so he can never be rich! He's created his reality.

SCOTT: And while there are greedy rich people, there are many more who use their wealth to help others, aren't there?

HARV: Sure. Who builds the hospital wings? Who donates the cancer diagnostic equipment? Who pays 90 percent of the tax burden?

SCOTT: You have another program called Life Directions. Tell us about that.

HARV: Life Directions helps people understand why they're here on this planet, and we put a package and a vision together. A lot of people teach about having a mission, and some people teach about having a vision, but we're the only one I know who ask, "What's the use of having a mission if you don't have the vision to make it happen in the real world? And what's the use of putting it out in the real world if it's not done successfully?" That would be like doing this book to try and help people and then selling only six copies. You need to live your mission. Once you discover your mission, it's useless until you put it into action in the real world, in a way that works, so it's sustainable and contributive in the highest way possible. And that's what we do.

SCOTT: I think when you're consistently seeking, that opportunity presents itself.

HARV: That's true. I believe in the idea of constantly learning. That's the way I created success. I came from a background that wasn't very successful, and learned my way to success. The difference between me and most other people is that I put it into practice in the real world. I'm not a trainer by trade. I was a businessperson, and I wasn't doing too well. I learned my way to success and reprogrammed myself. As you know, I joined Millionaire for only two and a half years, and it has just grown exponentially ever since. You've heard the saying, "Success is a learnable skill." I don't just believe that. *I know it!* I always say "Every master was once a disaster" meaning that everybody who's good at something now was once terrible at it. Take the greatest golfer or

Olympic skier. At one point, he or she was terrible at their sport. Everything is learnable.

SCOTT: You also make a point about using your natural talents.

HARV: Absolutely. Your mission is naturally going to be a part of your natural talent. You've got to really take a look at that. But you talked about being a seeker. Ninety-eight percent of the people out there are seekers. The problem is that there are not too many *finders*. I would much rather be a finder than a seeker. We teach that in our program called "Enlightened Warrior Training." The warrior doesn't go in to seek. If he's going in to seek, he's going to be dead on the battlefield. A warrior goes in there to find, and to win. People who are mediocre and middle class go in to see if something's going to work. People who are rich go in to make it work.

SCOTT: There seem to be a lot of people who are professional seekers, otherwise known as seminar junkies.

HARV: Exactly. That's what I'm talking about. But the people in my seminar are very different. I tell them, "Look, you're not here to take a seminar. You're here to change your life." I care what happens to you on Monday morning, what happens to you when you go in the real world. That's the only reason I'm doing this. It's not an exercise in exercises. It's an exercise in making certain that your life changes the minute you walk out of here.

SCOTT: I love your philosophy you presented. Can you share it with us?

HARV: Yes. It simply says: "Bless that which you want." It's supportive to admire the things you want. There are ways of thinking that are supportive to your success, and ways that are non-supportive. Most people have non-supportive ways of thinking. We help them make changes so their natural way of thinking is supportive to success.

SCOTT: Simple, really.

85

HARV: Yes. Successful people admire and model rich and successful people, don't resent them. Poor people are the people who resent them. "Bless that which you want." If you see somebody with a beautiful home, bless that home and bless that person. If you see someone with a beautiful car, bless the car and bless that person. If you see somebody with a great business, bless the business and bless that person. Because if you don't, and if you negate it in any way, shape, or form, you won't have it. If you think ill of someone who has a beautiful home, that means subconsciously you believe that other people will think negatively about you if you ever have one. So you'll never let yourself have it.

SCOTT: I'm sitting here in Dallas, the plastic surgery capital of the world, thinking about personal experience with people who are so jealous of others.

HARV: They'll never have success. It's finished. They don't even have a shot at it. When you can look at a limousine driving by you and give them love, you're in good shape. When you look at a limo and think, "What a jerk" you're finished. You'll never be in a limo unless you rent one!

SCOTT: What one last concept would you like to pass along?

HARV: There are several of them. First of all, I think that everyone is a "*Giant.*" The only thing that stops you from being a "giant" is your own mind, your own thinking process. A lot of people are into positive thinking. I'm not. I'm into "power thinking"! Positive thinking says everything is positive. It's a very la-la way of thinking. It says that there is no negative, nothing bad, and all that stuff. And pretty soon the mind gets sick and tired of that, because you're fooling yourself. Power thinking says there are two sides to everything, a positive and negative side to every situation and every person, because of the Law of Duality. Knowing that, I choose to focus on the empowering side of the equation, instead of just saying that another side does not exist. Knowing that I'm not fooling myself empowers me and helps me stay motivated and successful. Now I could choose to focus on the other side, which is just as real as the positive side, but it doesn't really help me. I'm going to choose the side that's empowering because it helps me live a better life, not because it's more true. Both are true.

SCOTT: Remind me of your joke about the lion, the monkey, the snake, and the elephant.

HARV: There is a lion coming along the path in the jungle. He comes across a monkey, and says, "Hey, monkey! Who's the king of the jungle"? The monkey says, "You are, sir. You are"! And the lion says, "That's right. Don't you ever forget it"! He keeps walking and he comes across a snake, and he says, "Hey, snake! Who's the king of the jungle"? The snake says, "You are, sir. You are"! The lion says, "That's right. Don't you ever forget it"! The lion keeps walking along the path, and he comes across a great elephant. He says, "Hey, elephant! Who's the king of the jungle"? The elephant just keeps on walking. The lion says again, "Hey, elephant! Who's the king of the jungle"? The elephant just ignores him. The lion gets mad and with his claws slashes the elephant on the butt. The elephant gets angry, picks up the lion with his trunk, and bashes him against the ground over and over. Finally, the battered and bloody lion finally says, "Hey, you don't have to get mad just because you don't know the right answer"!

Of course, that's all about people not wanting to admit what reality is.

SCOTT: Do you think most people are like that?

HARV: I do. They don't want to admit that they're not doing as well as they'd like, but they don't want to do anything about it. They think there's nothing they can do, and they think they have to figure it all out on their own. But the reason they're not doing as well as they'd like to be doing is because their way of thinking is not leading them in the direction toward making the choices that create real success.

The biggest gem I can give people is that it's not really about positive thinking, or even empowering thinking. It's just about understanding that your mind is the only thing that can take you out! The only thing that stops you is your conditioned-mind, the part of your mind that holds non-supportive conditioning. It leads to decisions that are not fruitful and don't achieve what you want.

If you want to change your outer reality, you have to change your inner reality—changing it so your natural, automatic way of thinking leads to success. What if you could think like Donald Trump?

What if you had Donald Trump's files when it comes to success? Your success would become natural and automatic.

SCOTT: That's right!

HARV: That's what we do. We revamp the files so that your normal way of thinking leads to success!

SCOTT: That's great. Thank you!

- To help support the United Way, obtain information and make donations, go to http://national.unitedway.org , or call 214-978-0000.
- To learn more about Harv, go to http://LearnFromHarv.com .

Tom Falk
More than Rich on Paper

As CEO of Kimberly-Clark, the world's largest paper products company, Tom Falk answers to plenty of masters—Wall Street, his employees, the market. But his real boss is the customer, and he's focused on more than just how to get them to buy more toilet paper. His mission is to make life better for millions. He shares a little bit of that commitment with us.

SCOTT: Kimberly-Clark is an amazing company, with revenues of about $16.7 billion in 2006. What is it like to have both the opportunities and responsibilities that go along with leading such a company?

TOM: It's a terrific opportunity to be able to lead a company that's been around for more than one hundred and thirty years. It's a great legacy, it's a great heritage, it's a wonderful group of people, and I'm just very pleased and proud to have the opportunity.

SCOTT: Kimberly-Clark's mission is to enhance the health, hygiene, and well-being of people every day, everywhere. That's a fairly ambitious promise. How do you ensure that you deliver?

TOM: Fortunately we make products that people need every day, whether you're talking about diapers, or bathroom tissues, or products in a healthcare environment. The good news is about a quarter of the people in the world use our products every day. But that means three-quarters don't! So there's still a great opportunity for us.

SCOTT: Nice to have that worldwide market, isn't it?

TOM: You bet.

SCOTT: You have a very large and diverse business. It's broken into three main areas of concentration: personal care, consumer tissue, and business-to-business. How do you achieve an industry leadership position in each of these?

TOM: The process starts with insights about the people who use our products. So whether that's a mom buying diapers, or a surgical nurse buying healthcare products, we really need to understand them, what they need, and what we have to do to meet and exceed their expectations. If we do that well, we're going to be the leader in every category that we're in.

SCOTT: How do you then translate that information to ensure that leadership?

TOM: Once we understand their needs, it takes innovation to bring new and improved products that really deliver value to these people. So, it's more of a technology business than we think.

SCOTT: That makes sense, because obviously toilet paper and tissue have been around for a long time. How do you provide innovation in that kind of marketplace?

TOM: By starting with consumer insights, we're bringing new products to the marketplace. We brought a new bathroom tissue with Aloe and Vitamin E. We've had all kinds of diaper innovations, whether you think about Little Swimmers, which are for kids at the pool in summer, or Good Nights, which are for children who have bed-wetting issues. There's a huge range of consumer needs that we can bring additional product capabilities to.

SCOTT: I would think as our society changes, the potential demand for an item changes. Do you have teams that are constantly looking at consumer demands?

TOM: Well, demographics affect a big part of our business. For example we spend a lot of time and energy on our adult incontinence business, because as the population ages, you know that certainly will be a factor.

SCOTT: You're following Wayne Sanders, who recently retired as Chairman and CEO. What was his legacy to your 130-year-old organization?

TOM: Wayne was a terrific leader. He was CEO for a little over ten years. And he really continued our transformation into a more focused consumer products organization. We had an airline business, an airplane refinishing business, and we had some other unrelated businesses that he got rid of over the years. He also did more than forty acquisitions of consumer operations around the world. So he really helped shorten the focus of the company during his ten years.

SCOTT: Did that set the foundation for today?

TOM: Absolutely! He left the company in great shape, and gave me a good opportunity to take it to the next level.

SCOTT: How do you envision Kimberly-Clark going forward?

TOM: It's my job to really transform the company. I think every good CEO has got to approach the job that way. We're spending a lot of time focusing on new capabilities. How can we do a better job of focusing on our customers? How can we move faster globally? Today we run more of a regional organization. We're trying to move to become a more global organization. It's my job to leave this company in much better shape than I got it from Wayne. So I'm up for the challenge.

SCOTT: You've got 64,000 employees. How do you keep them engaged in the overall vision?

TOM: People want to play for a winning team. You and I have both been involved in athletics, and everybody feels good being on a winning team. So one of the key objectives for us is to make sure we're communicating with our people, that we're sharing our successes with them so they really feel that they're part of a team that can win in the marketplace. And we give them the tools to go make it happen.

SCOTT: How are you able to translate that message in Malaysia, as well as in Europe, as well as in the United States?

TOM: There are a lot of really new communication tools that help. Every quarter I'm doing a short videotaped message that can be pushed to the desktop of every employee worldwide. We're sending out newsletters that continue to communicate with employees. And I pack the suitcase and go on the road. I'm in every region of the world several times a year, meeting with our employees and telling them about the great things that are going on in this company.

SCOTT: That's got to be exciting!

TOM: That's the most fun thing I get to do. Spending time with the people in the organization energizes me, and I hope it provides some energy for them.

SCOTT: For the last two years, Kimberly-Clark has been named on Fortune's list of "100 Best Companies to Work for in America." What makes it such a great company to work for?

TOM: Our business culture has four key elements: exceeding expectations, superior performance, teamwork, and caring for others. I think that last element of caring for others sets us apart from a lot of other companies. That's why we made the list in the past.

SCOTT: Are there any particular programs or things that the employees can point to, to say, "We really do feel cared for"?

TOM: Yes, one thing we do is encourage them to give back to the community. So we make a $500 donation if an employee or any one of their family members volunteers thirty hours in a year at a local charity. That makes them feel good, because they see we care about what they're doing, and what they're giving back to the communities they live in.

SCOTT: I think that's something that Corporate America should adopt. I hope you don't mind if we recommend "borrowing" the idea.

TOM: I stole it shamelessly from IBM. I think the more people who do it, the better for society. It's a terrific program.

SCOTT: I've heard it said that Kimberly-Clark has the fundamentals, the talent, and the opportunity to lead the world. Can you expand on each one of these?

TOM: I think I'd start with the talent, because nothing happens without the best team of people. So you've got to have good people, motivated to attack the opportunities. Then you've got to have some basic capabilities. You've got to really be good at understanding the consumer innovation, and driving those innovations into the marketplace. Those are key capabilities that we work on developing.

You've got to be in a business where there is growth. We've got great businesses that still have a lot of growth potential. When you put all those things together, it's a great opportunity for success.

SCOTT: Your products are manufactured in forty-two countries and sold in one hundred and fifty countries. How do you keep things running smoothly?

TOM: Well, again, it starts with the best people. And where we've been the most successful is where we've had strong management teams. If you go to Korea, we've got just a phenomenal team that has built that business from the ground up. You can see the same thing in Mexico, in Brazil, in Colombia. There are tremendous global business managers who know their market, get those consumer insights, build their customers, and really feel like they own the business.

SCOTT: Does the Korean management team see the Kimberly-Clark opportunity as part of a global organization, and therefore as a Korean company? Is that where that commitment comes from?

TOM: That's the delicate nature of being global. You want to get consistency around some big ideas, but you want everybody to feel they have a chance to contribute. The Korean team has got a lot of great ideas in a lot of areas, but they're also stealing shamelessly from other regions to find good ideas. The challenge is to avoid letting national pride get in the way of a great solution. You want to find the best ideas in the world, and drive them as fast as you can, wherever they came from.

SCOTT: Are those different processes transferable from country to country, with a localized tweak? How does that really happen?

TOM: Well, a couple of things. If it's a process, one of the things we try to get better at is measuring the process. If you had looked at a lot of companies, including us, five or ten yeas ago, everybody measured everything differently. There was great safety in that because you could only be compared to yourself. So, if you did a little better this year than last year, it was good enough. Now we've got a common way to measure waste, and speed, efficiency, and delay. Then we look at the top ten and bottom ten in the world and try to understand why they are that way, and learn from each other so we can reduce the gap between our top and bottom performers.

When it comes to the consumer, there are unique issues in some markets. In Korea, moms are more concerned about skin health. Having a breathable diaper was important for them. In every part of the world, you have to do some research to understand the different tastes to address in product design. They are real and relevant, and you've got to incorporate them. Breathable diapers in Korea led to a product improvement in the United States several years later.

SCOTT: Are there many ideas that come from the rest of the world back to North America?

TOM: That's the whole idea. More and more of that's happening. Five years ago it was mostly a one-way street, where we were selling stuff that originated in North America, to the rest of the world. But now we've got global teams put together. For example, we were making an advertisement for facial tissues and had a team of people from North America, Europe, Asia, and Latin America. They all sat together and bounced ideas off each other. What came out was a global piece of work that no one country owned, but everybody had a stake in.

SCOTT: Are there any products that are just absolutely particular to a country or region?

TOM: You'll find some things that are. Tastes can be very different. In Germany for example, consumers like very thick, very strong bathroom tissue, and they don't particularly care if it's soft. So four-ply bathroom tissue in Germany is pretty unique in the world. You don't see four-ply tissue anywhere else in the world. There are a few tastes like that where you find that consumer preference has evolved and taken a company in a whole new different direction. In China, you'll find the diaper category is very small, because children don't wear diapers. So it's not that you're trying to commit someone to go from cloth to disposable—they don't wear diapers at all.

SCOTT: Is it possible then to penetrate that market?

TOM: It's much more of an education process. Particularly in China where there are a lot of North American and European consumer companies trying to tap into that billion-person market. Consumers are exposed to a lot of new ideas and new products. It's just going to develop a little bit more slowly than in other parts of the world.

SCOTT: Kimberly-Clark also plays a large part in giving back to the communities where you're located. How did the give-back commitment get started?

TOM: It goes back many, many years. We've always had a feeling that the company should give back to their communities. The roles of the companies are to provide jobs and to give some support to the communities that their employees live and work in. So, for as long as I've been here, and many, many years before, we've always had a consistent policy of giving back wherever we operated.

SCOTT: You contribute significant philanthropic aid to organizations and programs that do their part to provide vital information, resources, and services to strengthen today's families. What programs do you support?

TOM: Our charitable giving is really focused on families, because most of our products are used by families at various stages. We just think the family is a critical element in society that needs support, and needs help. So we've done a number of things supporting the YMCA in North America, to help drive some of their family outreach and education programs.

   We have a partnership with UNICEF supporting a program for child-headed households for AIDS victims in Africa. Here again is a very different family unit, but our support is more focused on that. We're a very large United Way giver, where we match every employee's United Way contribution dollar-for-dollar, because a lot of it goes into family-oriented programs. We're a pretty big sponsor of the Boys and Girls Clubs, which again promotes better family situations.

SCOTT: These are all corporate initiatives, aren't they?

TOM: Yes.

SCOTT: They are supported by Kimberly-Clark itself on behalf of the communities, the countries, and the employees?

TOM: Right.

SCOTT: I know you personally serve as a National Trustee of the Boys and Girls Clubs of America. How did you get involved with the Boys and Girls clubs?

TOM: I moved back to Dallas a number of years ago. Wayne Sanders was and is still a trustee of the Boys and Girls Clubs, and he got me involved in some fundraising. I'd been involved periodically in prior years, and I helped raise funds for one of the clubs in Wisconsin. I just got to know some of the people in the Boys and Girls Clubs. I went out to the clubs, met some of the kids, and talked to some of the people who are working in those programs. There is just such an important amount of work to be done, and it was just something compelling for me to get involved in.

SCOTT: What are your responsibilities as a National Trustee?

TOM: In these types of situations, your main responsibility is to help raise money. They've got a lot of good people who are coaching the kids, and helping them with their homework, and setting up food bank programs. They've got a phenomenal gang intervention program and a food-for-grades program, where if a kid shows up with a B on their report card, they get a bag of groceries to take home every night. So they've got some terrific programs, but those programs need money. So we host the biggest fundraiser for Boy and Girls Clubs in the country. A lot of our friends and suppliers participate. We have them come down, invite them to the dinner, or we have a cocktail party for them afterwards. I have breakfast with them the next morning. In a good year, we raise between $1.5 million to $2 million. That's something we all are pretty proud of.

SCOTT: What do the Boys and Girls Clubs really need nationwide to be successful?

TOM: Well, they have a national budget, and they have local budgets. The national budget really helps upgrade programs at a lot of the clubs. So if they're going to set up personal computer centers, they have some funding to do that. They've got partnerships with Microsoft, and Compaq, and other suppliers to do some of that. The National Organization does a lot of federal grant work to help open new clubs in disadvantaged areas. But once they get the club started, they want the local club to be self-sustaining. So the local clubs do fundraising as well. There's a Dallas organization, Forte Verde, that builds partnerships with other institutions in the community and tries to help them be self-sustaining.

SCOTT: Growing up in Wisconsin, I've known the Kimberly-Clark name for years. Are there any other causes or anything in particular that you'd like to call to everyone's attention?

TOM: We talked about families. That's the big cause we're about. We've got to, as a country, make sure we're doing the right thing to strengthen the family so we don't lose an entire generation. We have to make sure we have the next generation of talented young people coming along.

SCOTT: What one pearl would you like to pass along?

TOM: Well, the pearl for me is that in the end it's all about people. If you don't have the best people working for you, and if you're not spending time motivating, and coaching, and selecting them, you're never going to accomplish your goals, no matter what you're trying to do. If it's in charity, or government, or business, it's not about the computer system, or the money, or anything else. It's about having the best people, and that's what will help you win.

- To help support the Boys Clubs and Girls Clubs, obtain information and make donations, go to www.bgca.org, or call 404-487-5700.
- To learn more about Tom, go to www.kimberly-clark.com.

98

Doug Caporrino
In Training for the Sport of Living

No one would have expected a sickly, chronically ill runt kid to turn out to be a champion bodybuilder, trainer to the stars, and advocate of total body wellness. Then again, few people are like Doug Caporrino. With a fiercely positive attitude and an entrepreneur's eye, Doug turned his Hollywood set security business into a fitness and wellness empire. He talks with us about the sources of his inspiration.

SCOTT: Doug Caporrino started our interview by reading a letter.

DOUG: Dear Doug, Thank you for giving me the tools to get where I've gone in my life. Your motivation and determination has truly inspired me to keep meeting the challenges that are put before me.

I guess I should start from the beginning so you will have a better understanding of my background. When my Mom was just three months pregnant with me, she underwent back surgery. The doctors were trying to convince her to abort the pregnancy fearing that the baby would not be normal, but my mom insisted on keeping the baby.

After my birth, I was diagnosed with three holes in my heart, and rheumatoid arthritis in my hands and knees. I wasn't allowed to participate in any sports for the first eleven years of my life in the hope that the holes in my heart would close. The doctors gave me until age twelve before they would consider open heart surgery. Lucky for me, when I reached that time, the holes in my heart had closed although I still had a heart murmur.

I was getting okay to participate in a limited amount of activity, and by age fourteen, I was given a green light to do whatever I wanted. Besides normal activities, I took up weight lifting. At sixteen, I was six feet tall and weighed less than 139 pounds. By nineteen, I had reached 230 pounds, through hard work, dedication, and lots of eating. But when I was eighteen and nineteen, I would run very high fevers and have severe bouts of diarrhea. I would lose fifteen to twenty pounds a week. The doctors would just say that it was the flu. Finally, one day, I was at home running a fever of about 104 degrees with severe vomiting and diarrhea. My Mom called the doctor, and he again prescribed some more medication. Later that evening my fever went to 106 degrees, and I started having seizures. My parents rushed me into a hospital, and they ran every test imaginable on me.

After two weeks, the doctors determined I had a rare disease called Mediterranean fever. There were only 756 reported cases in the United States at that time. The doctors started treating me with antibiotics. The side effects were usually severe stomach cramps, headaches, loss of appetite, etc. I allowed them to treat me for a few months, and then refused to continue. I was determined to build up my body and immune system on my own.

I remember meeting a chiropractor at the gym where I worked out, and was really intrigued about what he did. I always knew the body was amazing, but when I found out that you can tweak things a little to help the body heal itself, wow! I started seeing the chiropractor on a regular basis, and although I can't say for sure whether it was the antibiotics, or the adjustments and my nutritional supplement program, I have never had a relapse.

Later on in my twenties, I developed allergies. They would get so severe at times that I would seek medical treatment, and I was put on a few different types of medications to alleviate the symptoms. One of the attacks became so bad that I called the doctor from home, and he prescribed yet another medication. Well, the first medication interacted badly with one of the other medications I was taking. I became unconscious and as close to death as one could get. I remember waking up in the emergency room with black dust all over my body from the charcoal that was being pumped seemingly into every orifice to neutralize the effect of the drugs. If it wasn't for a very close friend of mine looking in on me, I wouldn't be writing this letter right now.

From there, I went on a mission to cure these allergies naturally. I tried everything from acupuncture to hypnotism. I finally came into contact with a chiropractor who practiced various motion techniques, and after a few short treatments I was practically cured. Once again, the body's own ability to heal itself amazed me!

Around the same time, I was getting ready for a national bodybuilding competition. I was just one week away when I became a victim of a hit and run accident. It left me with two crushed knees. But two surgeries later and after many months of rehabilitation, I was able to work out again. I was determined that I would overcome this minor setback, and I went on to win the national bodybuilding competition the following year.

I've found that people come and go in your life, but a few leave a lasting, profound effect. You have been one of those people. Two others are my mother and my wife. During my mom's lifetime, she underwent twenty-seven major surgeries including four total hip replacements, three abdominal surgeries, one shoulder surgery for bursitis, a hysterectomy, three bouts with cancer, and eventually kidney failure. She recently passed on, but continues to live within me. I feel her presence with each race I do, pushing me to bike a little faster, or to run a little quicker. She convinced me that I could achieve anything! My wife now holds that position. She is the most inspirational person in my life. Her undying compassion and need to heal people is a rare gift. She has been told she has hands from God, and I must agree. You see, she is a chiropractor.

I hope this letter is useful, and that it may give someone that extra push to succeed in whatever they pursue.

The author of the letter is Doug Caporrino.

SCOTT: That's absolutely amazing!

DOUG: That's my story. I often tell it at the talks I do, because when people see me walk into a room, they think, "How he can possibly relate to a romance, or whatever I'm going through right now?" So, when people understand that I'm just as human as they are, they are able to hear my message a little bit clearer.

I've faced a lot of challenges, but that is exactly how I look at it, Scott. These were really just challenges in my life. I literally came as close to death as someone could, and if it had not been for a very dear friend of mine looking in on me—actually it was my dog—I wouldn't be here.

SCOTT: Talk about "man's best friend."

DOUG: No kidding!

SCOTT: Now to one of your passions—I discovered a fitness video that you did years ago. What was that all about?

DOUG: First, let me say that Jay Leno has nothing to worry about. This is going back about twelve or fourteen years. It was called Doug

Caporrino's "One Day at a Time," and I approached fitness and nutrition as an addiction—people get addicted to bad exercise and eating habits. To change their thinking we took people through a special course. Every single day we just educated them a little bit more about their body so they would learn what their body was capable of, and what they could do.

What I did, unlike anybody else in the market at the time, was create a monthly lottery for people who purchased the video. We would pick a person who had purchased the video that month, and I would go to their home personally. I would be their personal shopper as well as their fitness trainer for three days. They really got a better understanding of exactly what they needed to eat, how to read food labels, and the proper way of exercising. It was very interesting and a big education for me as well.

SCOTT: Great concept! Did those opportunities come to you through your Hollywood set security business?

DOUG: Yes. I started the security company while I was in college, and ended up getting the contracts for any movies that were being shot in New York, Pennsylvania, or Connecticut. At the time I had the opportunity to work on my first movie, *Night Hawks*, starring Sylvester Stallone and Billy Dee Williams. I was able to strike up a relationship with Sly Stallone, and one thing led to another, and before you knew it, I was training him for *Rocky 2* and *Rocky 3*. So, it was certainly a great opportunity, and that led to another opportunity. Then came the sequel to *Saturday Night Fever*, *Staying Alive*. They needed somebody to work with John Travolta, so I had the opportunity to work with him as well. Before I knew it, I had the label of "trainer to the stars." Then I became the health and fitness consultant for the Joan Rivers Show in the morning and worked with Joan for about a year or a year and a half. It was just absolutely tremendous!

SCOTT: Not long ago, I had the pleasure of going through one of your workouts, and it kicked my butt! I was able to identify muscles I didn't even know I had. Is that pretty common with your workout?

DOUG: It is. The thing I love about that particular workout is that people look at it and think, "I need some type of huge piece of equipment in order to get results." But you really don't. It's really just getting in tune with your body, and as we did in that class on the physio ball, just using different muscles than you normally use. It's a humbling experience. When I first got certified in the training on the physio ball, I said, "Oh my God, I can't believe I'm getting this kind of workout just out of a big blown-up beach ball, which it appears to be, but it's much more than that.

SCOTT: You are the Vice President of Fitness and Nutrition for a company called, "Creating Wellness." How did that come about?

DOUG: About two years ago, my wife went to a program called "Total Solutions," which was given by the Chiropractic Leadership Association, headed by Dr. Patrick Gentempo. It's a three to four day boot camp of chiropractic medicine. They take you to this mountain in Colorado and show you how to use this technology that they call the "insight machine." It's essentially a surface thermal EMG scanner that looks at the spine. My wife befriended Dr. Gentempo, and they started talking about dogs, strangely enough. He was looking into purchasing one, and she said, "You know, you really should meet my husband—he has a very special interest in dogs."

That night we went to dinner together and I liked Patrick immediately. There was just an atmosphere of mutual interest and respect, one of those love/love relationships. Patrick told me he had envisioned establishing a company to educate people about wellness. He needed someone to be the fitness trainer and nutritionist, and come up with all the different formulas to provide people with an individualized program suited to their needs and goals. He asked if that was something I would be interested in. Quickly, we got it all down on paper, and it was really just a match made in heaven.

Patrick's vision was for a chiropractic office, let's say, Jones Chiropractic, to become Jones Chiropractic "Creating Wellness" Center. It's a customized approach to wellness. Someone would walk in and get a totally individualized program, from customized menu planning to customized nutritional supplementation and customized exercise programs all recorded on CDs or DVDs. We also offer a custom software program called, "Creating a Wellness Coaching System." Patients come for a ten- to fifteen-minute coaching session every week with a professional that we have trained. We do a lot of problem-solving.

103

For example, during a session, let's say as a patient, I was to walk into the office and report, "Scott, I'm having problems with my menu planning this week." We'd go to the audio section of the software program, punch in the problem with the menu planning, and identify several viable alternatives. We would then burn an audio CD for you on the spot, you listen to it on your way home, and it gives you an individualized menu, associated information, and even exercises to focus on that week. It's really light years ahead of anything that has been out there on the market.

Another thing that I love about it is that it actually addresses all three dimensions of negative stress in people's lives—biochemical, physical and emotional. My philosophy has been if I can't fix what is between a person's ears, I could never fix their bodies.

We just launched our program and have eighteen centers right now. We are going to be opening twenty centers per month for about the next six or seven months.

SCOTT: You're also President of Results Through Research. Tell us about RTR.

DOUG: After going to my first couple of chiropractic conventions, I asked who was teaching the chiropractors about fitness and nutrition. There wasn't anybody. Now you can go in and make an adjustment, but if you don't look at a person from a biochemical or physical standpoint, they're going to continue having the same problems. So I came up with the idea of creating this company called Results Through Research. We create a monthly audio subscription series that teaches doctors and the laypeople about nutrition. Each month I interview either a sports celebrity or entertainment celebrity, and see what has worked for them. So every month it's new, it's in an audio magazine format, and it's been a ton of fun. It's probably just about a year and a half or two years old right now, and we are currently the fifth largest audio subscription carrier in the United States.

SCOTT: With so many plates spinning at one time, how do you keep things running so smoothly?

DOUG: Focus and discipline! It's really about delegating. I've been able to attract an incredible team of people who work with both companies. I have been very fortunate to learn how to create teamwork over the years in all the different businesses I've been involved with, and I think that plays an important role. As I have always told anybody who works with me, in order to make any *dream* work you have to make the *team* work. You have to be able to communicate effectively, and have an open forum for anyone working with you to share ideas and possibly implement something that might benefit you and the company.

SCOTT: I know a portion of your time, talents, and resources are dedicated to philanthropic pursuits. What cause would you like to call to everybody's attention?

DOUG: I have been lucky enough to work with an organization right now called the Achilles Track Club in Manhattan. They are now all over the world and have different chapters in almost every state. They are especially big in South America right now. The Achilles Track Club is for handicapped runners and handicapped athletes. Of course, if you said that to them, they would probably take off one of their prosthetics and club you with it, because they really just see themselves as challenged.

These people are just amazing! They are truly inspirational! I tell my clients who lack the inspiration or the motivation to really follow through with their Wellness Program, to go stand at the finish line of any marathon. Don't go when the winners are coming in, but when the handicapped runners start coming in. And bring a box of tissue. That's when you see people who are blind being led across the finish line, or people in wheelchairs, or those running on two prosthetics. That will make you say to yourself, "My God, can I look myself in the mirror and honestly say I can't get up in the morning and exercise"? Because these "handicapped" people do it day in and day out. They have the most tremendous amount of fortitude and drive, and don't see themselves any different than anyone else in the world. They have been just an amazing inspiration to me!

SCOTT: Well said! What one last lesson would you like to pass along?

DOUG: The greatest thing that I've learned is to use every experience— good, bad, whatever it might be—as a learning experience. There are no failures in life, only lessons to be learned. If something doesn't work out, take what you can from it. Take a step back and reflect on what just happened. Look at what you could have done better, and don't repeat the same mistake.

Life is really just learning. If you're open, and you check your ego at the door, you recognize that this is a learning experience for everyone. You become better at identifying what to do in the next set of circumstances, so life continues to get better and better.

- To help support Achilles Track Club, obtain information and make donations, please contact www.Achillestrackclub.org or call 212-354-0300.
- To learn more about Doug at www.resultsthroughresearch.com.

Trip Kuehne
Amateur Golf's Proud American

You could say golf is in Trip Kuehne's DNA. After all, his brother, Hank plays on the PGA Tour, while his sister, Kellie, plays on the LPGA Tour. In fact, the entire Kuehne clan could be considered Dallas' golfing royal family. But there's more to Trip than chasing a little white ball. He's a man who believes firmly in education, in supporting research into a disease that's affected a beloved family member, and in his faith.

SCOTT: Trip, the Kuehne family has been a golfing institution in the Dallas area for as long as I've lived here. Who is the driving force behind the family's love for golf?

TRIP: I would have to say it's me. I was reading the *Dallas Morning News* at the age of nine or ten, and came across an article talking about the Dallas City tournament. I had never played in a golf tournament before, and I begged my mom and dad to let me play, so they got me a set of clubs. I went out, played, and lost in the semifinals to a guy who's now a golf agent by the name of Brian Newton. It was a five-hole match and he beat me three and two—I lost as badly as I could possibly be beaten. But a love and passion was created.

I played all the other sports. I was the quarterback in football, the point guard in basketball and sports came very naturally to me. Golf on the other hand was very difficult. At the time I started to play golf, my father joined the Sports Club in Las Colinas. At the time, each family member had their own individual membership. At eleven, I came out and had an interview with Director of Golf, Scott Erwin. I had hit some balls for him and had a sit-down interview. They allowed me a membership, and I developed my passion for golf.

Because I was playing golf, my little brother (Henry—now on the PGA Tour) decided to take up the game. My little sister (Kellie—now on the LPGA Tour) at the time was a nationally ranked tennis player and ice skater. Kellie decided she wanted to be with her brothers on the golf course. We all started playing because we loved being around one another. Before we knew it, we were winning tournaments. The rest is history.

SCOTT: Recently, a picture of your family surfaced from 1988 with you all standing together at the Four Seasons Resort and Club. What's it like to grow up in a family with such a passion for the great game?

TRIP: It's lots of fun! Not only do we have passion for the game but for each other. I can't ever remember a football game or golf tournament or a school activity that I didn't have either both parents there and my siblings, or at least part of the family there, to support whatever the activity was. We're a very close-knit family. I think in large part because of that, we've been able to accomplish so many great things.

SCOTT: You've had an outstanding amateur record. What are your fondest memories?

TRIP: I have so many fond memories, and some as an amateur did not come from my playing. One of my fondest memories is caddying for Henry when he won the 1998 U.S. Amateur. To see what Henry had been through with his recovery from alcoholism at nineteen years old, and then being there with him on that big day. To watch him play to the best of his ability and win was an unbelievable feeling.

As far as me individually, the 2003 U.S. Open comes to mind. Winning the national championship with my team members at Oklahoma State was amazing. Winning the state high-school individual medal as a senior and also winning as a team—having my brother on the team with me. I have so many wonderful memories. The ones I really cherish were the ones I could share with other people—whether with my brother, or my teammates at Oklahoma State.

SCOTT: In the 1994 U.S. Amateur you played against a young Tiger Woods. What's it like to go toe to toe with Tiger?

TRIP: It was great! That week, I played extremely well. Until recently, it was probably the best week of golf I've ever played. My father was my caddie, and I look at it as a week where a twenty-two-year-old could spend his time with his father.

As far as the final match with Tiger, I birdied seven of the first thirteen holes, played great, and shot 66/73 and lost to arguably the greatest player of all time. It was neat because I had a personal relationship with Tiger prior to that match. He was probably best friends with my brother and sister on the AJGA junior tour growing up. Most people don't know, but the first time that Tiger traveled without his father, he came to Dallas and stayed with my family to play in an event here at the Las Colinas Sports Club.

I was in the most pressure—packed situation I had ever been in to that point, and I was able to rise to the occasion. That's the memory that I take from it.

SCOTT: Trip, you played on the 1995 and 2003 Walker Cup teams. What does it feel like to represent your country in such a prestigious match?

TRIP: It's what every amateur golfer strives to do—make the Walker Cup team and represent your country. It's an honor. One of the reasons I rededicated myself to golf in 2001 is because I wanted that experience again. Both Walker Cups I've played in have been on foreign soil. The feeling is indescribable when you're on foreign soil and your national anthem starts playing. When the flag went up, I got goose bumps. I remember in Wales at the '95 cup, I looked down at my arms and my hair was standing straight up! You have a sense of pride and accomplishment by being there.

SCOTT: This year you were the low amateur at the U.S. Open. What was that like?

TRIP: Unbelievable! I was sitting there thinking back to the first professional event I played as an amateur, which was the Byron Nelson in 1991. I played the first six holes and remember seeing all the people. Thank goodness for me there was a rain delay because I was six over after six holes. When I came out the next day, I never saw any of the people. And it's been that way ever since. I've never seen the people unless I want to.

I can remember Saturday at the U.S. Open. I had just shot sixty-seven the second day and I was playing with Justin Rose, one of the young guns from the European tour. He's ranked in the top thirty in the world. I'm teeing off on Saturday at the U.S. Open and I looked over at my caddie, Mike Tyler and said, "Man there are lot of people here today." I saw the people and didn't play very well on Saturday. There I was, teeing off on Saturday knowing if I had a great weekend and shot a pair of sixty-sevens the last two rounds, I could win the U.S. Open!

I've played in two U.S. Opens and have been fortunate enough to make the cut both times. To me it's the ultimate test in golf, because the golf courses really challenge your golf game. But the U.S. Open challenges you as a person, too. The conditions get harder every day, and it challenges you to deal with your emotions. It's the ultimate in golf because it's the best players in the world. Everyone below a certain handicap has the opportunity to qualify. There are basically no free passes—you have to earn your way there.

To have the finish I did, to be low amateur and finally get a USGA gold medal after so many second place finishes, was an unbelievable feeling—to know that my game stacks up with some of the best golfers in the world.

SCOTT: At the 2003 U.S. Open, you had a drive recorded at 419 yards. Anyone who loves golf knows what an accomplishment that is. What does it feel like to hit a ball that far in such a prestigious event with the best players in the world in the same field?

TRIP: It tells you what happens when you're performing at the optimum level. It happened on the seventy-second hole. Believe it or not, I really didn't try to do anything special. I stood up on the tee box and I vividly remember my only thought was to take a deep breath, so I took a deep breath. I thought I could turn on it and just try to get into the fairway. When you hit the fairway, the hole gets pretty easy from there.

Everything lined up and all was perfect! When the ball left the club, the trajectory was just like I wanted it. It started out just in the right spot and it ended exactly in the spot I was looking at. It was everything I wanted to do to get myself into a position to be the low amateur. It was like it all came together in that one shot. I did something that I'm not sure that I could ever duplicate.

SCOTT: You also played well in the 1995 Masters. What's it like to play Augusta in the Masters?

TRIP: It was another unbelievable experience. It was my first major as an amateur. Unfortunately, I got all caught up in the hoopla of the event. I got there way too early on Saturday prior to the tournament starting. I played too much golf; I left my best game at the par-three tournament because I became exhausted, being so excited to be there.

I remember going over the hill at number eleven and seeing Amen Corner for the first time. I got goose bumps. I thought to myself, "This is Jack Nicklaus, this is Nick Faldo, this is Greg Norman, this is Ben Hogan, and this is where the greatest golfers in the world have walked. And this is where it either starts to unravel or where somebody picks up and makes a charge."

The way they treat you at Augusta is second to none. They go out of their way to make you comfortable. It was a fantastic experience. One of my goals is to earn my way back there someday as a player. That's why today, when its thirty-five degrees and raining, I'm out hitting balls. It's also one of the reasons I stayed amateur—to prove to myself that I can go as an amateur and play well at Augusta.

SCOTT: What keeps you motivated to work so hard at the game?

TRIP: I really don't look at it as work. Golf is a game. You're supposed to have fun. I'm a lot like the way John Wooden was about playing basketball. I really enjoy preparing, I like to get out there and practice. That's what drives me. I feel that I've played better the last couple years because I've really dedicated myself to the game of golf.

SCOTT: You play out of the Four Seasons Resort and Club in Las Colinas. It's the home of the Byron Nelson PGA tour event. Has Byron himself ever given you any advice?

TRIP: We've talked on numerous occasions. He had a very big impact on me when I was about thirteen years old. At the time he was helping Tom Watson with his game. Tom was actually in town for a lesson and I happened to be at the range. Afterwards, I got to play a few holes with them. He said to me, "Trip, you know you're doing pretty well. If you continue to work on your game, maybe one day you can beat me."

So there I was, a very impressionable thirteen-year-old, and here's the number one player in the world at the time, Tom Watson, getting a lesson from potentially the greatest player of all time, Byron Nelson, and they told me to work hard on my game. I needed to be out there doing what they were doing.

111

That was one of the reasons why I started playing again competitively. I referred back to my passion for the game, and got my game back. I try to show that passion to all these young guys whose future is the PGA Tour. I try to let them know that they shouldn't just take advantage of the game. If this is going to be your living, love it and live it to its fullest. Most important, respect it.

SCOTT: Your brother Hank and sister Kellie play professionally. Have you ever have any aspirations of playing golf professionally?

TRIP: Not really. I tore my shoulder during my sophomore year at Arizona State. At the time, I was ranked the number one college player in the country, ahead of Justin Leonard and David Duval. I was at a point in my life that should have been the happiest because I was playing great golf. It was then and there that I decided something was missing. I decided I wasn't going to focus on just one thing. I found that focusing on academics, having a good social life, having a good golf game and being loyal to my family and friends was far better. I never really dreamed about playing professional golf. That's one of the biggest differences about making it on the PGA Tour and not.

For example when Justin Leonard and I were twelve years old playing together in tournaments, all he talked about was playing professional golf. I'm of the opinion that if you have two people with equal skills and talent, and one has passion, that's the one who will be successful every time.

I dreamed about living in Dallas, Texas, playing golf, working on Wall Street and being with my family. Life on the PGA Tour wouldn't have allowed that. My family is too important to me to do that. I think it's actually a great lesson for anybody.

SCOTT: Not only did you get your degree from Oklahoma State University, but received your MBA with honors as well. What drove you to continue your education?

TRIP: I've always held the opinion that no matter how rich or how poor you are, your education is something no one can take from you. I've always lived by the motto that if you're going to be someone, you might as well be the best you can possibly be. Luckily I was given some talent, some brains, and the ability to study and focus. I graduated in the top 10 percent of my high-school class. School came fairly easy to me.

When I tore my shoulder, I realized that I might never be able to play golf again. My goal from that day forward was straight "A's." I only made one B after that, in managerial accounting.

One of the goals I have for my later years is to either be a golf coach or an athletic director. I want to be directly involved with the athletes so I can influence the lives of young people. Anybody who's highly recruited or goes to a big conference school tends to think that when they're signing their scholarship, it's a stepping stone to the professional ranks. As we both know, that's just not the case. The odds of making it to the professional level are unbelievable.

The one thing you can do as a coach or athletic director is guide young athletes and make sure they get an education. If you have an education and have a great mind to fall back on, you always have a chance in life. At the end of the day, I don't have to just rely upon my golf ability to make money. I could make money the rest of my life by using my brain.

SCOTT: You're an equity adviser for Legg Mason in Dallas. How did you choose the investment world as a career?

TRIP: Our family always took trips to New York City when I was younger. At thirteen years old, I basically fell in love with the stock market. We took a trip down to the floor and the paper flying around fascinated me. I was amazed by the construction and destruction of wealth that could happen via Wall Street. I always knew in the back of my mind it was something I wanted to do. It was a passion I developed very early.

My first experience in the investment community came in the fourth grade. Our math teacher had a stock-picking contest. The way we got our money or credit to invest in the stock market was based on how we did on our quizzes and tests. I won that contest. Ever since, I remember picking up the business page, looking up the various symbols and seeing where stocks were, what the market did. I recognized it was something that I wanted to do.

I originally went to work for a company called White Rock Capital. I was an equity analyst for a hedge fund. I learned how that side of the business worked and how to research companies. I'd really like to be able to have my own fund someday, whether it is a mutual fund of funds or a hedge fund.

About the time I rededicated myself to golf in 2001, some friends were called by Legg Mason to open a new office in Dallas. They asked me to join them, so I did. I'm an equity adviser now and it's fun. And I'm seeing it from a totally different side of the business.

SCOTT: What is your specialty?

TRIP: I'm in institutional sales, so it's mutual funds or hedge funds. I'm able to use the training I got at White Rock. I specialize in smaller cap stocks and also a little bit on the short side of the business. I'm able to do research on companies and point out flaws in their balance sheet or where things don't add up.

SCOTT: How has golf helped your career?

TRIP: I've made some tremendous contacts through golf. It's one of the great things about playing golf and then going into business. Many times I've been able to pick up the phone, make a call, get some name recognition, get to CEOs, and ask questions. If it wasn't for golf, I wouldn't have been able to spend two hours on a driving range with Jack Welch, former CEO of General Electric.

SCOTT: Is one of your passions to support junior golf and see the great game grow?

TRIP: I definitely want to see golf grow, and I help in any way I can. I'll help the zero handicapper or Saturday hacker. I just want them to love the game the way I do, and respect the time-honored traditions of the game. It drives me crazy watching some of these young kids when they're practicing wearing headphones. I don't like the fact that people are carrying cell phones on the golf course.

Golf should be about having four hours to go play and really enjoy the game, having fully taken in the experience. It's what it's all about. The only problem I have with the game is that it takes a fair amount of time to play a full eighteen-hole round. It's harder and harder to find the time to carve out the four hours to play.

Junior golf is something that I believe in because it starts to create that passion for the great game. Golf is a lot like life. I know that I'm not as good as that eagle or birdie, but I'm not as bad as that bogie or double bogey. I'm somewhere in between. You can learn a lot about a person on a golf course, because through four hours and eighteen holes you're going to have highs and lows. You get to see how people handle both extremes. It's a game that every day you get to share with other people, and it offers the chance to create lifelong friendships. It's one of the things that makes it so special.

SCOTT: What cause would you like to call to everyone's attention?

TRIP: The one that's dear to my heart is the Juvenile Diabetes Research Foundation. My sister is a diabetic and was diagnosed when she was ten years old. Tom Barton, a gentleman I used to work with, and I are the co—chairs of Kellie Kuehne's "Teeing It Up for a Cure" golf tournament each year. Over the last five years we have raised almost five and a half million dollars that goes straight to diabetes research. With the money that is being raised and the continued research it funds, one day we will find a cure. I hope and pray every day that we find a cure.

One of the best female golfers in the world is a girl named Michelle McGann. She's been so afflicted with diabetes she's having an extremely difficult time just trying to play any more. She's definitely not playing to levels that she's reached in the past. It's hard because I watch Michelle and see what she and Kellie have gone through. Kellie has done an unbelievable job tackling diabetes. She's never once complained about it or felt sorry for herself. She realized having diabetes is something she needs to manage and live the very best life she possibly can.

I heard a report recently that of children born in 2001, one out of three will develop diabetes. That's an epidemic. Everyone knows someone whose life has been touched by diabetes or its effects. Finding the cure will impact the lives of children and their families so many can live a much happier and productive life.

SCOTT: What one last belief would you like to leave with everyone?

TRIP: First, I feel we all need to be true to ourselves. I define being true to yourself as finding something that you have a complete passion about and following that passion with all your heart.

Second, preparation is everything. Learn to love to prepare. The successes you have are rewards from hard work, dedication, and being prepared. My father used to quote the old Vince Lombardi line, "The harder you work the luckier you get." I really believe that. If you've prepared by paying attention to the details and have been consistently working on the fundamentals, you are equipped to handle any pressure situation.

Finally, get to know the Lord. It's one of the great things in my life—a rededication to our Lord. He already knows what He has in store for us and if we follow His Word and follow His plan, He keeps us out of trouble. I know I'll be very successful because of my faith. No matter whether it's a success here on earth or the ultimate success—knowing that when my time here has passed the doors of heaven are going to open up.

I'd like to be remembered for my place in golf as a person who loved and respected the game. That anytime I went to do battle I gave it my all, and when it was over I was the consummate competitor—a man of character and somebody anybody could genuinely call in time of need, and that I would help in any way possible.

- To help support the Juvenile Diabetes Foundation International, obtain information and make donations, go to www.jdrf.org or call 800-JDF-CURE. You can also e-mail the Dallas Chapter at dallas@jdrf.org.
- To learn more about Trip, visit his professional Web site at www.doubleeaglecapital.com.

Art Sellinger
The "Art" of Long Driving

Two-time National Long Drive Champion, Art Sellinger could have contented himself with the golfer's Holy Grail—bombing a little white ball farther than any other man in the United States. But that wasn't enough for this Dallas, Texas, resident. Through his own personal "treat people right" code, a tireless work ethic, and an eye for opportunity, Art translated his long drive success into business success becoming the CEO of Long Drivers of America (LDA). Even more important, he is using his success to raise money to win the battle against a condition that affects his family: autism.

SCOTT: How did you develop a passion for the game of golf and hitting the ball long?

ART: When I was ten years old, I can vividly recall watching the Masters on television. It was the first golf tournament I ever watched and probably the best Masters ever played, between Nicholas, Miller, and Weiskopf. Nicklaus made a big putt on sixteen. We had been living in Las Vegas and my dad would go and play golf on the weekends with his friends. He was not a very accomplished player, but he loved the game. My brother and I started tagging along and that's when I really took a liking to the game.

At that time it was pretty easy to get involved in junior golf. The movement was just starting. My brother Saul, who was bigger and stronger at twelve, did a lot better at the game than I did. He was really the player of the family all through his junior high and high school days. I developed a lot later.

We had one set of clubs that we shared between my brother and me. I think we bought them at a garage sale. They were Hazel Hicksons, and I couldn't tell you if they were ladies' or men's. Saul got the even numbered clubs and I got the odd. All the specifics about the game we learned as we went. We had no formal instruction. We taught ourselves until I was about seventeen years old. I look back and treasure those experiences with my brother and my father on the golf course.

SCOTT: I read that as kids you and Saul would work consistently to out-drive each other. Is that where the long drive passion started?

117

ART: We cared a lot about who hit the longest drive on each hole. He was bigger so he would hit it farther most of the time. He was a very long hitter. When he was fifteen or sixteen, he could hit his ball three hundred yards. This is in the 1970s, with the way equipment and balls were back then. That's amazing! I could never keep up with him. Our long driving "competitions" kept up even when we moved to Houston.

That was 1985, the year before I won my First National Long Drive title. We even competed against each other at the district finals. Then in '86, I actually defeated him. Only the top two got to go to the national finals, and I was the one who knocked him out. That's really about the time his long driving days ended. We went head-to-head quite a bit, and it wasn't until I was about twenty years old that I was equal and finally hit farther than he was hitting.

SCOTT: You won your first long drive championship at age twenty-one. How did that change your life?

ART: Golf has always been in my blood ever since I can remember. But when I won the National Long Drive title, I was out of golf. I was in the hotel business. I was going to be a hotel manager. I was learning all the different areas of hotel management.

I got some time off from work, went to the National Championships—and won it! Winning gave me an opportunity, plain and simple. It didn't mean I was going to be on the PGA Tour, but I looked at the opportunity at hand and I tried to formulate a plan.

This was the only time, from 1975 to today's current event, that there was no television coverage of the event. 1986 was the year they lost their television contract. Without any television coverage, nobody had really seen me win. If I was going to do some exhibitions, I was starting without the power of television showing my win. Publications wrote stories, but they were here and gone pretty quickly.

I figured I had a year to capitalize on the opportunity before me. I was the first player to win with a metal driver, made by TaylorMade®. I felt like that was an opportunity in and of itself. The rookie in me thought that some agent would come along and make my life very easy. In fact, I met an agent and for the first forty days, I waited for him to do some agent stuff. But the phone wasn't ringing. I had already quit my job because I had won all of $15,000 and at age twenty-one, I thought I was the richest guy in the world. But nothing was happening and I was just playing golf every day. I was working to make myself better because if I was going to be in front of all these people I needed to hone my skills.

SCOTT: Sounds like your game was improving but not your prospects. What did you do?

ART: I picked up the phone and called TaylorMade® and talked to the president of TaylorMade® at the time, Gary Adams. Then I fired my agent.

Gary had heard that I had won the National Long Drive title. I told him that I loved my TaylorMade® clubs and had used them since I was a junior in high school. I confirmed that I had won the national championship using a TaylorMade® club, and that if there was anything I could do to spread the word about his company, I'd certainly be interested in doing it.

He said that he'd like to meet me at the PGA show. We met, we had a sandwich, and he was the nicest guy I ever met in my life. He said he'd like to give me a six-month trial, do a few exhibitions and a few promotional things. Well, my six-month trial ended up lasting fifteen years!

SCOTT: With the TaylorMade® endorsement contract in hand, how long did it take to make the "Art of the Long Drive" come to life?

ART: You don't realize how many years it takes to market yourself. That first win changed my life to where everyday I could wake up and promote Art Sellinger. At that time, I thought of it as a business—I was basically a machine to be sold for events, corporations, what have you. I felt I had the opportunity to become a business, but needed to be promoted. So we promoted me as "an added attraction to enhance anybody's event." I've never felt that I'm the most important part of the day, but rather that I could do something to add to the enjoyment of an event.

I did about twenty events in 1987, about thirty to thirty-five days of travel. I remained an assistant pro at the Northwood Club. I had an arrangement with the head pro for me to go do my events when scheduled and come back to my club duties when appropriate. At twenty-two years of age, I could make $40,000 hitting golf balls and come home and be an assistant pro at a club—it was great!

SCOTT: It was after your second Long Drive Championship win that you went full-time into the exhibition business. What was that transition like?

ART: In 1988, I did probably forty exhibitions and that's when it really started becoming a full time endeavor. In 1989, I signed on with Vinny Giles of Pros Incorporated. If they found events for me I did them, but I still did my own thing as well. The TaylorMade® relationship was in year three, and I also picked up Ram golf balls and Sandvik titanium shafts as sponsors. I knew it was my responsibility to meet as many people as I could, because I knew that some of these people would say, "Hey, this is a pretty good guy and a good entertainer." It's cool for people who have never seen a golf ball hit over 340 or 350 yards. But once you see it, what else are you going to do for me?

The desire to show people more caused me to start hitting fewer drivers and more entertaining shots. Those exhibitions afforded me the opportunity to meet over 150 PGA Tour players and the top golf teachers.

SCOTT: You've done nearly 1,700 exhibitions in twenty-four countries. Are there any that stand out?

ART: The stuff that stands out was being billed with some top PGA Tour players. That was very flattering and humbling. When I did the opening exhibition for Junior World in 1989 and had the opportunity to stand in front of those kids along with a couple of tour professionals doing a clinic, that was really memorable.

I think the thing that was the most flattering was doing corporate events, for years real big-name companies were using top tier talent to entertain their best clients. That was very gratifying. I was working very hard, traveling 230 days a year, and this was in a time of no e-mail, no cell phones, none of the technology we have today. It's very difficult to run your business by payphone.

I've done some very neat things. I stood on top of the twenty-seven-story Pan Pacific Hotel in Vancouver, B.C. and hit golf balls in the Bay trying to set a distance record. I've hit golf balls over rivers, done some weird things, and even did a few things I'm not real happy with. But I've learned from them all.

Doing exhibitions for U.S. troops in Korea was definitely a highlight. My day consisted of doing four exhibitions on four separate bases. I was shuttled around by an Army Blackhawk helicopter around Seoul. It was extremely exciting. It was great to be able to do that for the American troops. Being able to hit a golf ball a long way has obviously afforded me a lifestyle and an opportunity to meet some very wonderful people. All my closest friends have come through the game.

SCOTT: You have done exhibitions for Ford, IBM, GTE, and Sun Microsystems to name a few. What does it feel like to perform for such major companies for their largest customers and prospects?

ART: It's important to me because they chose me. Still to this day, when a company calls me to be that added attraction, they know that their customers will be at ease. I work with Fidelity Investments, taking their top customers around Augusta for the Masters. The company is counting on me to maximize their experience.

Golf is the only true Pro-Am game out there today. You can't play football with somebody, nor hockey with somebody, nor basketball nor baseball. Golf is your only real choice when it comes to using a sport to truly entertain. Even a high handicap player can end up feeling great about his game because there's always a highlight in a round.

I always work hard to make those folks feel special so that they will walk away and say, "I had a great day"! It's important that they feel I was a good guy, and not just there for the money.

SCOTT: Why do you think that way?

ART: You have to, because you're making an incredible amount of money for a day's work. I've made as much as $10,000 in a day. But I've seen Tour Pros who make $35,000 in the day and act terribly toward the people who retained them. These guys are trained to shoot a score playing golf inside the ropes, not necessarily entertain. But I'm trained to entertain, and that's what I do. When the event ended, I always wanted the client to say, "good dude, good guy, boy he really cares, I really had a nice time and he hits some neat shots." If the only thing they say is he hit the ball well, I didn't do my job.

If somebody puts their trust in me, it's my job to return that through my efforts. I've always felt uncomfortable being thanked. I don't think you thank somebody that you pay. If I've donated my time, that's different, thank me a bunch. If I'm working with twelve customers at the Four Seasons, then I deliver the Four Seasons experience just as Mr. Nelson would give himself. I have to be just one more piece of the puzzle that makes that particular experience just that much better.

SCOTT: You've really made the sport of long driving what it is today. How does that make you feel?

ART: Being a full-time competitor from 1986 until 1993 was everything for me. It really kept my career going. To win a couple times and knock on the door a couple other times is a great experience. It's a shame that in the past long driving didn't have the arena that it should have or the media support that it deserved. It was always a grass roots event with one division. With the LDA today, we have multiple divisions with far more participation and excitement. It's so cool! Companies sell their products based on distance and power. It's the most exciting part of golf. How far can you hit it?

When *Golf Digest* came out in 1993, I felt that long drivers could possibly have a new arena, and that's when I got involved full force. We found out in 2004 that it truly is a sport. We had over thirty hours of coverage in 2004. It's a passion because kids just eat it up. They watch it on *television*. They want to hit it big. Even the seniors love it! We went from one division to eight divisions. Now we have people come across the pond to see if they can do it. It's happening right before my eyes, and it's a growing, living entity. I'm so glad that I'm running the sport as a former competitor, because I appreciate where it came from. We work to give the player what I didn't have when I was at my peak. We give fans an incredible value when they come to watch the event. It's a critical time in the sport's evolution and we're very excited with what's going on.

SCOTT: A couple of years ago you opened Sellinger's Power Golf. How did that come about?

ART: I was tired of paying rent. As with many entrepreneurs, you just want to be in more control of your destiny. I wanted to own the building that housed the LDA. I found this building we are sitting in, a mile from my children's school, two miles from the house, very convenient for me, and made the purchase. A logical thing from the LDA standpoint was that when somebody came into the sport, they had the opportunity to buy the specialized clubs needed for competition.

I also didn't see anybody really out servicing the golfing community with anything other than price. Something has been missing in the process, service. If a customer needs a driver to a certain specification, we can do that. If we sell a wedge to someone, we can insure the loft and lie are perfect for him or her. We're just trying to do things a little differently. Our policy is that if we build you a club and it doesn't improve your experience, we'll build it again. There aren't many people doing that. That's the way I've always run all my businesses—it's the little things.

Ultimately, it's another spoke in the wheel of everything we are doing around the game of golf. We have the LDA, the Pinnacle Challenge, the Art of Long Driving which manages players, we do corporate hospitality and then of course, Sellinger's Power Golf. I've always said I need to have multiple opportunities working at once. I guess I learned this growing up in Vegas. It's like playing craps—as long as you were winning three ways and losing two, you were doing fine. You just can't bank on one area because if you get a bad roll, you're done!

SCOTT: You've worked with the Ronald McDonald House, the Multiple Sclerosis Society, the Children's Miracle Network, as well as others in their fund-raising efforts. How has this been rewarding to you?

ART: I want everyone to understand that I was compensated for those appearances. From day one, if I did all the charity requests I received, I wouldn't make anything. This was difficult when I was told the other professionals were coming without some type of fee. It had become a delicate balance. I created a program where I would discount fees or even find a sponsor for my portion of the day. That way I could perform, I could survive, and the charity could benefit by the enhancement I provided to its event.

There are so many charity events that provide the same package—a goodie bag, here's your lunch and let's go play. But by enhancing the event through a long driving exhibition, we could attract more players and raise more funds. I did always pick six events per year that I did for free. After the exhibition, if they wanted to put me out on the par-five, I would hit a tee shot that the foursome could decide to use in return for an extra fee for the charity. It was another way to raise more money for charity at each event.

I get one of my biggest thrills with kids that are underprivileged. This year I probably did twenty shows for underprivileged kids through the First Tee program. I also did another one with my dear friends from Wall Street that pay for this camp for kids that have cancer. I gave lessons to terminally ill kids. I've been in the trenches with stuff like that and I've seen it work to give them hope. It's very rewarding and it's very touching. Because I do this for a living, I did the best I could to add meaning to their desires.

SCOTT: Can you give us an understanding of why the LDA supports the Autism Society?

ART: We have Autism in our family with my son Zachary. We found out he was in the spectrum at two and a half years old. At that time, we were not very knowledgeable about Autism, so we became very involved in many local programs through his school. It's a tough deal because there is no pill, you don't even find out why it's happened. So you don't want to get involved in chasing brain scans and things like that. He is in the good part of the spectrum. There are kids way worse off than Zachary. It's been an education process for my wife, Shelly, and me.

The opportunity afforded itself for the LDA to have a couple of additional events that would be bonuses for the players while funds could be raised for autism. For the last couple of years, we have put on events in New York and Dallas to raise money for increasing awareness and additional government programs. In only a few years we've raised close to $100,000 through the tournament, and we were able to donate $40,000 personally. I wish I had more time in the day to organize more events.

This charity is special. For example, after you've donated your first $15,000, the executive director flies out and has lunch with you and your wife. Many other charities are multi-million dollar situations. Autism has not yet gained the notoriety to achieve those kinds of donations. We're bringing it to the forefront as best we can. For anyone to send $40,000 or $45,000 to the Autism Society, they just have no understanding of what a huge difference that can make. Any little bit of awareness goes a long way to help the Autism Society.

This is really a national issue. They need the help of the National Institutes of Health in Washington, D.C., to detect this in kids early. With early intervention, we can help people learn to function at a much earlier age. That will ultimately reduce the situations where forty- and fifty-year-olds are in homes unable to take care of themselves. Hopefully my son, through the efforts of the Autism Society, will be able to hold a job and have a fruitful life. We don't know at this point, but we're very hopeful.

Today, fifty families will learn that their child has some form of Autism. That's 350 families a week, 18,250 families per year. It's a staggering number. When we first learned, we were so scared. We just didn't know—we couldn't communicate with a two-and-a-half-year-old. We don't spend our day wondering why any more. We spend our day trying to research what can be done to make his life as high-quality as possible.

The Autism Society needs the fund-raising to grow consistently. It's part of the LDA plan this year and will be for years to come. Many people have helped in these fund-raising efforts, including my sponsors at Titleist, Pinnacle, Cobra and many others around the Dallas-Fort Worth area. They have been wonderful in donating money to this cause.

SCOTT: Is becoming aware of a disease like this also producing a consciousness to do something about it?

ART: Yes. The Autism Society is so unique. We came to recognize this because of Zachary's situation. Even the smallest contribution makes a huge difference because of limited funding and limited awareness of this disease. A $30,000 or $40,000 or $50,000 donation might afford them the money necessary to hire another employee. There's a tremendous opportunity to help! It's rare that relatively little dollars stretch such a long way.

SCOTT: Is there one last point you would like to leave us with?

ART: I truly believe that you have to look at everything that comes your way in your life as an opportunity. At that point, we have the choice as to what we will make from it. I hit a golf ball long enough on October 7, 1986, to claim my first National Long Drive title. That alone meant nothing—I found that out soon. Using that event as a steppingstone was

125

a totally different animal. I was able to create a fantastic working relationship with TaylorMade®—that in turn allowed me to develop a business through exhibitions—which allowed me additional Long Drive tournaments and eventually, owning the Long Drivers of America.

Opportunities come in all shapes and sizes, and it is up to us how we use and develop them. My pearl has to be to take those opportunities that come along and run with them—you'll be glad you did!

- To help support the Autism Society, obtain information and make donations, please contact www.autism-society.org or call 1-800-3 AUTISM.
- Reach Art at www.sellingerspowergolf.com or www.longdrivers.com .

John Dealey
International MasterMind Expert

John Dealey is known to many as the world's leading expert on the MasterMind process today. But in reality, John's ventures range far and wide beyond this expertise. He's working to allow everyone he meets to reach their full potential by sharing his talent, developing a place of service to others, and encouraging them to achieve "their" success. His philanthropy, while many times anonymous, is inspirational to say the least. This son of the Dallas, Texas frontier is a man with a story to tell.

SCOTT: John, I've known you for some time now. Your heart and knowledge have always amazed me. Please tell us a little bit about yourself, just to give everybody a little bit of background on who you are and what you're all about.

JOHN: Thank you. I'm very fortunate in that I come from two frontier families. My mother's family first came to Texas over a hundred years ago while Texas was still an independent nation. My father's family came shortly thereafter. And I was raised with the marvelous history of those images. I started my first business when I was nine years old and became a self-made millionaire at age twenty-seven. I have changed industries and have done that again, and again, and again. And now, my mission in life is to be of service to people and their "honorable designs," to help others enrich their lives and be a "small part" of assisting or inspiring them to achieve their dreams,

SCOTT: What industries have you been involved in?

JOHN: I've always been an entrepreneur. At age nine, I told my father I needed a bigger allowance and he said "No," so I started my first business selling golf balls. I became the wealthiest kid on the block and that gave me my first taste of success! After college, I became involved in the retail shoe industry with the Earth Shoe business which, thanks to the power of a MasterMind, is where I first became a millionaire. I have also been involved in investment management, insurance, business consulting, and I'm founder of the MasterMind Advisory Councils here in the Dallas, Texas, area.

And now I'm committed to teaching the marvelous power of the MasterMind principles to the greatest number of people possible, for the benefit of all.

SCOTT: That's certainly one of the ways I've come to know you as well. What is the power of the MasterMind?

JOHN: Well, I am a great believer in the power of stories and I think maybe the best way to answer your question is with a story about Andrew Carnegie. He came to this country as a very young man with two powerful and unique goals. One was to become exceedingly wealthy in the first half of his life, and the second one was to give all that money away in appreciation to America for all it had done for him. When Carnegie accomplished the first of those goals he began to wonder how it happened. So he made an agreement with a young reporter at the time, a young guy named Napoleon Hill, and they engaged in what we in modern day language might call a joint venture.

Napoleon Hill was to go around and interview the 550 presidents of the largest corporations of America around the turn of the century about a hundred years ago. And basically just ask them one question, "What is it that's made you so successful"?

It took Napoleon Hill two years to do all those interviews. When he brought all of that research back, they went through it together and Carnegie was able to summarize it in two phrases. He said: "If you would be exceedingly successful in this life: 1) Know very clearly where it is you want to go, and 2) Be a member of a MasterMind group."

MasterMind is the power Carnegie and Hill discovered and named that helped Carnegie, Ford, Firestone, and all those great men reach such high levels of success. Hill explained: "No two minds ever come together without thereby, creating an invisible, intangible force, which may be likened to a third mind." The thoughts, energies, and passions of the individual members of each "MasterMind" group unite into a larger energy—the third mind that Hill talked about. The power of the MasterMind comes alive as the individual members of the group bounce their thoughts and ideas off each other. It is a magical, wonderful, and exciting process!

SCOTT: Exactly how do you define a MasterMind group?

JOHN: A MasterMind group at its simplest is just two or more people who come together and share from their combined knowledge and wisdom about a topic that they're focused on. Napoleon Hill defined a MasterMind as people meeting together for a definite purpose, with mind and body coordinated in a spirit of harmony, working toward a common goal.

Actually, most of the groups in the world that can be considered MasterMind groups are not called "MasterMind" groups. They are called power teams, focus groups, brainstorm sessions, boards of directors, think tanks, study groups, discussion groups, and more. Mark Victor Hansen often calls them dream teams, and says the true power of one plus one is *eleven*. MasterMinds are more like the fish of the sea. They just they come in different sizes and different colors and different shapes, they move a different speeds and they're just totally different all over the world. In a MasterMind group at its very simplest, people take pieces of information and ideas and, by working together, the extra energy of the MasterMind helps them create something even bigger and better than the sum total of all those parts.

SCOTT: Can you give us some examples of MasterMind groups?

JOHN: Boards of Directors in business can be MasterMinds, The PTAs at your schools are actually MasterMind groups, as are many study groups and religious organizations. One of the largest and most successful Christian Churches in the world is in Asia with over a hundred thousand members, and they don't even have a building. They do everything with MasterMind groups of about four to six to fifteen people, although they don't use the word MasterMind, they call them cell groups. And also, a MasterMind group can be something like my Advisory Council groups for business owners. We have been meeting for over twenty years on a regular basis.

On the other hand, you can have a group of people who are lost without a map come together at a gas station and talk with the guy in the station for maybe two or three minutes. With all of them working together, they can combine their individual knowledge and come up with the right directions.

Also, in the classic movie *Apollo 13*, the group of the astronauts combined with the people on the ground formed what really was a

MasterMind group. That marvelous power is what came in and changed the entire focus to help solve the problem and save those men's lives.

SCOTT: Sounds like it's a really powerful tool for people to affect change.

JOHN: Absolutely, to affect change and also to help you stay on the path of change. Once you have your major purpose defined and you're going forward, MasterMind will help you stay on your path. MasterMind groups help you see things from other points of view. Don't block yourself in by thinking in only three dimensions. Add a fourth dimension by bouncing your ideas off your MasterMind group. That different perspective can give you marvelous new insights and inspiration.

Also, who doesn't like a challenge? As you see your peers succeeding in their business endeavors, you'll be even more driven to go out and make your ideas an even bigger success. You gain positive energy and motivation with each session!

Additionally, your confidence will go up as you enjoy these brainstorming sessions with other people who think like you. As your confidence level increases, so will your positive results. As your positive results increase, so does your self-esteem, personal satisfaction, and success!

SCOTT: That's awesome! Obviously you are totally committed to this process and are helping other people understand it and put it into action.

JOHN: Yes, I think my core center focus is to be of service and is mostly related to helping others learn to use MasterMind. And I do that because I have seen many, many examples of it helping people to bring marvelous positive changes into their lives. I see MasterMind as being more flexible and more powerful over a long period of time than anything else I have ever seen. The bigger mission is to be a part of the team of leaders and people who take, expand, and multiply the assets that we have to make the world a better place and to help even more people. Some of the world's leading experts have said we use less than 10 percent of our mind/spirit capacity, and my biggest goal is to help take that to over 80 percent. Certainly in my life and in others lives, the law of serving and of service, enthusiasm, and forgiveness and laughter, all of these things are very powerful. Also, helping others to increase their self esteem, which again I believe is very, very powerful.

SCOTT: That is pretty amazing.

JOHN: I love leverage on things like that. It has a chance to take somebody's life and completely change. Leverage combined with MasterMind can do it 24/7, for me to be of service for people 24/7 is another one of my strong drivers. To give people tools that continue to grow and then fit them is like the old adage from years ago about fishing—don't give them a fish, but rather teach people how to fish.

In addition to that, I like another old story about not giving people asparagus, instead teach them how to plant asparagus, and then the asparagus grows of its own accord. Asparagus is actually one of the incredible things in the plant world. It grows an inch a day. Giving people the knowledge of a MasterMind will help them grow at a remarkable rate every day.

SCOTT: And you're giving heart in your desire to see people prosper! It's amazing, and I've been the recipient of that and I thank you tremendously for that in our relationship. Over time, what is truly that driving force that causes you to want to invest at the levels you do in others?

JOHN: I don't know exactly, Scott. It just burns in my heart to be of service. I am fortunate to be able to participate in Jack Canfield's Transformation Leadership Council. To me, it's been a very influential MasterMind group. Being around people who are actively using their resources to bring marvelous benefits to the world has been a very powerful driving force in my life. I want to do things that are not just single, "one time" gifts, but rather something that will continue to give and give and give and give or even to give multiple ways. Historically, in the world of charity, one of the ways using has commonly been manifested is to provided a building—steel, brick and mortar, because it can be used to "give" all the time. My focus has been more on the human spirit. I love to give with something that has a chance of really going long-term.

SCOTT: You come from a family known for their support of so many through the newspapers and media and different holdings your family has. Was that a big part of your influence to do this, or was this something more internal?

JOHN: Oh, I don't want to say it was self-created or something from the air that I breathe, but I think it was maybe a gift to me in my genes, most definitely the environment I was raised in. My family's history of supporting others and bringing about positive changes to Dallas and the world, has certainly given me many great examples.

The lessons learned by my father as he studied under Dr. Norman Vincent Peale have been very influential. My mother also has taught me many, many marvelous life lessons that I continue to use and teach today. Certainly it has been an inspiration to be descended from Sarah Horton Cockrell, the first woman in the state of Texas to become a millionaire. The things that she did in her life against enormous odds are absolutely remarkable! My mother had a thirty year dream of getting the biography of Sarah's life published and we finally got done 2004.

Many people have read that book and they said, "This can't be true! It's just like she is this super woman of the frontier"! But her story is true, and her determination to improve her life and the lives of others can be a marvelous inspiration to anyone!

SCOTT: What's the name of that book?

JOHN: The book is called *Sarah—The Bridge Builder*. As of yet, it's not very well distributed, but we're working on that also. As a matter of fact, there's one woman who wants to make it a textbook for a course! It's about Sarah Horton Cockrell who came from Virginia with her parents and her siblings. I don't know why that touched my heart so. Anyway Sarah's parents brought their entire family with all of the children. Sarah was the oldest girl and as they came to Texas, they thought it was going to take them six weeks; as it turned out, it took them four months to get here.

And when they got here after a four month long trip after planning it for six weeks, you can imagine they were a little short on supplies. Sarah wrote to her beloved sister and said, "Well, we're finally here and we have heard that there is a settlement nearby and I hope that Daddy will find it soon and go in because we also hear that in the settlement that there is a store and we are in bad need of supplies. I'm particularly in bad need of paper so that I can write to you."

The next letter from Sarah to her sister, a few weeks later says, "Well, there is a settlement nearby. Daddy did find it. There is a store in the settlement. There are two log cabins. One of them has two rooms and in one part of one of those rooms is what they call the store. However the contents of the store were a little bit disappointing. I forgot that this was the frontier and I have a wonderful home in Virginia. And the contents of the store were two jugs of gin and a bolt of calico. And the name of the settlement is Dallas." So that's how the first of my family came to Dallas.

SCOTT: Other members of your family have been influential, not only in your life, but also in the history and growth of Dallas. Can you tell us a little about your great-grandfather?

JOHN: My great-grandfather was George Bannerman Dealey. His interest has today grown into a giant media company not as well known as many, but we own the Dallas Morning news, several radio stations, and nineteen television stations across the country. In 1895, Colonel Belo owned the largest newspaper in Texas in largest city in Texas. At the time, that was Galveston because the Galveston flood of 1900 had not occurred yet which caused it to go from the largest city in the state to nonexistent. Colonel Belo gave an award to my great-grandfather for twenty-one years of service. It was a dear award to him because twenty-one years of service is a very long time and Belo thought that it was like age twenty-one and many in our society when a person becomes an adult or becomes a man. The company still gives that award for service today.

SCOTT: Wow! That's pretty amazing history and obviously giving you some pretty amazing guidance and like responsibility or feel along the way.

JOHN: Yes. And George Bannerman Dealey was responsible for helping remove liquor advertising from the front page of the papers, in spite of people telling him that would ruin his business entirely. The front page of newspapers used to be nothing but ads, almost all of them liquor. Also, using the MasterMind principles with a fabulous group of businessmen, they changed the history of Dallas and of Texas and of

133

America. They helped build the levees here in Dallas. Before the levees, Dallas flooded two out of every three years and also to a lesser degree, for a few days every year.

Because of the cost, there was a lot of opposition to the levees and many said it was impossible, but my great-grandfather and the others kept focused on the flooding. They came together, raised money among themselves and hired an engineer that finally was able to get them built.

SCOTT: Wow, that's pretty amazing when you think back to how it's all come together, obviously it's been extremely fascinating to get to know you because you are an extremely private person. When it comes to support of philanthropic causes, what causes would you like us to recognize and also support?

JOHN: There is a wonderful movie titled *Pay It Forward.* Just think of all the marvelous things that would happen if there was some way that we could promote everyone giving more financially to charity on a much more regular and frequent basis. Also that they continue to give in other ways like time, physical labor, wisdom, maybe even web design, fund raising and more.

There is an old saying "little and often fills the purse" that can be put to very good use by everyone, regardless of their age or personal situations. Just imagine what could happen if everyone decided to tithe their money and their time, materials, laughter and love. What marvelous benefits could come from something like that!

SCOTT: What other things can we do to support philanthropic causes?

JOHN: Make a financial contribution to one charity a day. Your interests can be very broad. Another thing from one of my book series called *Words That Have Changed Lives.*

There was a story in there about a woman who was in a really bad way, had three kids under the age of five, had lost her job was about to lose her house and car. Her husband had left her and had beaten her—it was horrible story.

She was going through a fast-food drive-thru to get dinner for herself and the kids; she looks in her purse and realizes she doesn't have enough money to buy meals for all four of them so she buys food for the kids. She was just out of options. As she goes up to pay at the window

134

and the restaurant worker hands her the food. As she tries to pay for the food he says, no ma'am. She thinks somehow the guy at the restaurant knew she was in desperate straits and was trying to give her a gift. That's the only thing she can think of, either that or he's confused, anyway he doesn't know what's going on. What comes out in the conversation is that the car in front of her, who does not know her, paid for her meals.

SCOTT: That's easily an action each of us could take as we go through a drive-thru. Simply perform a total random act of kindness.

JOHN: Absolutely. What happened to that woman at that point where she was about to break, turned her spirit. It did something inside of her, and her life turned around and blossomed. To this day many times when I go through a drive-through line I buy the meal for the people behind me. When the meal is paid for, I give the person in the window two small cards that tell the story. One of cards is for the restaurant worker so he or she can hear part of the story too and understand what's happening, and the other card is to give to those who received the meal I paid for. The card explains why I paid for it and my hope that they pass along the good deed.

SCOTT: Wonderful! I love the idea of pro-actively supporting the "Pay It Forward" concept. Are there any others?

JOHN: Another group that is helping both women and children to recover from unhealthy situations is the Abundant Life Ranch near Kansas City. Their mission is to provide a place of hope, healing, and restoration for girls in physical and emotional crisis. They are doing marvelous work in helping others.

Also, these days, due to the unfortunate increase of drug, alcohol, and gang problems in our public schools, supporting alternative education for our youth is very important. Park Avenue Christian School in Springfield, Missouri, is one such school that is helping to make the world a better place one child at a time. They are a non-profit and are funded by donations, and work very hard to give each child an opportunity to learn in a positive, safe, and healthy environment.

SCOTT: Is there one last word of advice that you would really like to pass along?

135

JOHN: My mother taught me the values of love, laughter, joy, and peace. If we all work together, every day, to make the world a better place, we will have been successful—being of service, spreading laughter and joy, helping others achieve their dreams. Just listen to the small quiet voice inside of you, and you can begin by taking action, one small step at a time, each of us doing our part, being a representative of God's living spirit. Make each day a beautiful day, go in peace and live in joy.

SCOTT: Absolutely awesome! We turn our lives into something wonderful while helping others reach their full potentials. Thank you for your insights and wisdom!

- To help support Abundant Life Ranch, obtain information, and make donations, go to www.abundantliferanch.org, or call 816-721-0608.
- To support the Park Avenue Christian School, obtain information, and make donations, please contact http://pacschool.org, or call 417-865-9875.
- To reach John, contact him at www.YourAdvisoryCouncil.com.

Freddie Rick
BetterTrades Founder and Visionary

What's it like to have it all — and lose it —and THEN get it back again? According to Freddie Rick, it's a blessing! How did he do it? He surrounded himself with the best mentors possible in the field of expertise he wanted: trading in the stock market. After learning from his mistakes and regaining what he had lost, he created an organization dedicated to teaching others to accomplish the same money making skills and methods starting with the BetterTrades Market Essentials workshops. BetterTrades is now a top recognized leader in the field of teaching individuals to trade in the stock market. Freddie and his internationally acclaimed faculty at BetterTrades now teach a wide variety of courses designed to helping people learn to trade in ways that are best and most appropriate for each of them.

SCOTT: Freddie you've got an exciting story that we'd want to share. Tell us where you came from and where you're headed.

FREDDIE: I'm originally from Kentwood, Louisiana. When I got out of high school, I joined the Marine Corps, and eventually became a sniper. Of course, there's not much demand for that position outside the military, so after the Marine Corps, I got involved in the network marketing business. I did extremely well—was a millionaire at 29; had all the toys, the house, the cars, the boats, all the stuff; then, and at age 31, I was broke. That was the first huge lesson that I learned—if your priorities aren't in order, God will straighten them out for you fairly quickly, if you don't take the initiative to do so yourself.

SCOTT: So what did you do?

FREDDIE: I found myself kind of checking out of life. I went from the penthouse, to the nut house, to the jail house—I've been through all the houses. Then I ended up drinking very heavily trying to deal with it all. Finally, one day I just decided that nobody was going to look out for me other than me, and that I had to draw a line in the sand and start working on myself. So I quit drinking, sobered up, and started working on myself. That's when I started attracting other people into my life. I met my wife to be, Mitzi, and we started to develop a relationship over the phone—and one thing led to another.

SCOTT: So Mitzi helped you with this turn-around?

FREDDIE: Yes, Mitzi came down to visit me in Florida where I was living in a one-car garage. Somebody had helped me out by allowing me live in their garage. I can remember our first Christmas together. I gave her half of a five dollar bill—tore it in half and told her she had half of everything I had in life and that if we worked together, we could take it and turn it into a million dollars. I had one of those fake million dollar bills that I also gave her in her card at Christmas. Over the next several weeks and months, we were able to start trading in the stock market, but ended up losing the majority of her money in the market. We started out with $254,000, and I lost most all of that during 30 to 45 days of trading. It wasn't hard to realize that I needed to bear down and figure out what I needed to do to trade in the market successfully. Ultimately, we made all that money back and plus much more.

SCOTT: You've obviously turned everything around personally and professionally.

FREDDIE: Today, I'm financially better off than I have ever been in my life; and a lot happier with whom I am as an individual. It goes back to when we were basically living month to month, pay check to pay check, just giving—tithing every week. Mitzi taught me a lot about giving back, and believing and trusting in God. God was always there at the back door to provide when the need arose, and it was always just in time, not a minute too soon nor a minute too late. We just had to have faith and believe. It was amazing that every time that we needed some money, we had just enough to make it work, even though we were tithing, and giving money away that we didn't really have to give away in the first place. To this day, we continue to give and it's amazing how the more we give, the more we receive, and that we can never give more than we get back. It's kind of wonderful the way that works.

SCOTT: Mitzi stuck with you through some pretty tough times. How did you get in the stock market to begin with?

FREDDIE: I was in associated with a company that had just gone public. So I wanted to get involved but did not have the money. So, I ended up borrowing $2,000 from a friend of mine and put the $2,000 in a brokerage account. The day the company went public, I bought the stock.

The stock opened at $8 and ran to $31 in the first couple of hours. I was bit by the bug! To make a long story short, that company's stock got locked up the first day of trading. It never reopened for trading and ultimately went bankrupt. The friend that lent me the money actually lost that money. But here's the best part of the story: It was only recently that I realized he had lost that money. And I could never figure out why I didn't get called on the free ride. Then one evening Mitzi and I took my friend and his wife out for dinner – he told us that he had called to stop payment on the check to the brokerage company, but that they had cashed it already, so he lost all the money. I was completely shocked to hear this! So, I pulled out my wallet and gave him all that money back, right there on the spot. It was a great feeling to be able to do that.

SCOTT: That's great! You've said before that Mitzi funded your start in the market, and you lost the vast majority of her stake to begin with?

FREDDIE: She had $154,000 in her retirement account which was her life savings. She also had her house, which was completely paid for in full. She paid for us to go through the stock market education course. Then she took a $100,000 line of credit out on her house. With that $100,000 and the $154,000 in her retirement account, we started the process with $254,000. In the first 30 or 40 days, I would say I lost approximately $220,000 of that money, and, needless to say, it was gut wrenching!

It was a real tough time! At one time, it literally sucked all the energy out of me. I could not get out of bed. For five days, I just sat there in a daze trying to figure out what had happened. But Mitzi stuck with me.

SCOTT: So you decided to not bail out of the market but more importantly, really learned to use it as a tool. How did you go about that?

FREDDIE: I think getting pushed into the corner forced me to learn what I had to learn. A lot of people will have a bad trade or something

139

will happen in their life, and they will walk away—because it's just easier to walk away. Well, I couldn't walk away because Mitzi had trusted me with everything she had in her life, and I had just come out of a situation where trust was a difficult thing for me because of earlier life experiences. Here is Mitzi, a person who had trusted me with everything. Who was I, if I turned and walked away from everything and her, and left her hanging, just like what had happened to me?

I had to do something. So I read every book you could read on trading. I listened to every CD and watched every DVD I could find, and went to every related course that I could attend. Simply through the school of hard knocks, and trying the ins and outs of different strategies, I figured out what would work for me and how to be able to generate consistent income. I boiled it down to the Forest Gump way of trading.

I'm a very visual person, so I created a bunch of templates (I call them my Forest Gump sheets) of how to do the trade so I could see it on paper visually in front of me. I would stick them up in front of me in the little room where I was trading. I became a very visual trader; and that's when the turnaround began to happen. Actually, these templates that I created are in our workbook today.

SCOTT: Is that when you and Mitzi decided to share that knowledge with others, and created an educational organization?

FREDDIE: We did. Originally, we actually went to work for one of the companies where we had gotten some education. I had figured out some concepts that I wanted to teach which they didn't like because they didn't have the concepts. Basically, they said if I wanted to teach the things I was doing, that I needed to do my own thing.

So I opened a website called the "Gump Investor". We started sharing the knowledge and information we had with others. It started one-on-one. We took the concept into churches and called it Biblical Principles of Market Prosperity (BPMP). We started doing it for a love offering and shared all the information we had. From there, the "Gump Investor" website grew to a subscription. Then people would come and spend one-on-one time, in personal consultation with myself and Mitzi. BetterTrades has now grown to an annualized 60 million dollar company with thousands of happy students—"family members", as we call them – and now we have a couple hundred people involved in the company, working with us to achieve our goals.

140

SCOTT: What's the mission of BetterTrades?

FREDDIE: The mission of BetterTrades is to impact people's lives positively, help them achieve their dreams, and as an individual working in the company, to have fun doing it.

SCOTT: That's awesome! And you say that there are thousands of students and growing?

FREDDIE: I was just the springboard into gaining the knowledge that we have as a company. I went out and found others, the faculty, that had expertise in other areas of trading in the market. Those like minds working together create a third and more powerful mind. That's really what BetterTrades is: a melting pot of individuals that have phenomenal knowledge of how to trade in the market.

　　We give people the opportunity, a buffet of courses and methods, to pick and choose which trading strategies they like, and we offer a breeding ground of people that want to look at alternative ways of making money in the market. We have also created this environment to foster and grow our faculty members. Many have been students that came through the program initially and have become tremendously successful. Now they want to share their knowledge. They want to be around other people that have the same common goals and objectives.

SCOTT: And as they grow, does it give them greater opportunity and flexibility in their lives?

FREDDIE: It does! It allows them to share and give back, and it allows them to be gratified by being around individuals that like trading in the market and are enthusiastic about the same things. It allows them the ability to spread their knowledge as they grow. The whole idea of wisdom is to impart it to others. Our faculty love to see people grow.

　　The great thing about the market is that whether we teach 100, 1,000, 1,000,000, or 10,000,000, these ways of profiting from the market, never hurts anyone. It actually helps the whole economic process. People get to do what they love, and they make more money. Ultimately, they are able to grow and contribute more—it's a never ending circle—a force for good.

SCOTT: I know there are many people who have become some really great success stories and experienced life changing moments in using their new education. Can you relate some examples?

FREDDIE: Sure. Just last weekend, we had an event during which some people were sharing testimonials. I learned of a lady who gave her first $25,000 in stock market profits away to other individuals. She was there with one of the individuals she had given money to, early on in her trading career. That individual had, in turn, actually given money to somebody else and started them in the process. It's tremendous and so personally rewarding to see that happen.

Then we had a gentleman come and share with us his plans for the new church that they're building, and how they were funding it through the stock market. It was great to be able to see the plans, the drawings, and the blueprints of the church and now, ground has been broken for the church, and they're building it as we speak.

Another gentleman, a very high level professional VP with IBM for many years, related his story: He had never been on unemployment in his life, but IBM down-sized and cut him loose. He came and saw us six months ago at his first event, and he was just "paper trading" or doing "non-funded trades". He was a very stiff individual, seemed like the personification of a traditional corporate man. I met him again six months later. Now, and he and his wife had bought a brand new motorcycle, a Honda Goldwing. They are part of the Gold Wing Road Riders Association and now are travelling together. You wouldn't know it was the same guy! He told us that BetterTrades has truly changed his life, not only financially — their profits are up $270,000 over the last six months – but that now he is a person who is more relaxed, carefree and loving. You actually see a glow about him! I could go on and on.

SCOTT: Sounds like a lot about BetterTrades is giving people the opportunity to live by choice, as opposed to doing the things we have to?

FREDDIE: Well, it's about living the dreams that people want to live, instead of dreaming of the dreams they want to live. That's the true excitement of the opportunity, no matter what someone's dream may be.

SCOTT: It seems like a lot of students themselves carry out this philanthropic philosophy. Is that part of your system?

FREDDIE: We gave our business to the Lord Jesus Christ many years ago, and let Him do what He wanted with it. We also let people know that we are in it to continue to give, to help other people. When they see that, not just through Mitzi and me, but through all the members of the BetterTrades family, that desire to contribute continues to grow. It's like throwing a pebble in the water and seeing the ripple effect. I constantly use the phrase "pay it forward" from the movie many years ago. We always ask people to continue to "pay it forward."

A lady that came up to me in a recent event and said she didn't have the money to buy the tools that she wanted to buy. She showed me a picture of her 5,000 square foot house that had a $3,500/month mortgage. She told me her husband had died, and she was in tears, worried she was going to lose the house. She wanted to buy $4,000 worth of products, and I asked her how much she had. She had $2,400. She pulled out this book she had that said she needed to just pray about what she wanted, and make it known. So, I said, "Today's price is $2,400 for the tools and that book. But you have to write me an IOU in the front of the book that you will "pay it forward"—not to BetterTrades, but to somebody else who needs it once you become profitable and successful in your trading." So, she wrote it in the front of that book, crying big alligator tears the whole time. Her dreams came true that day. Those are the best kind of things to be able to do for people.

SCOTT: So, where does that giving heart come from?

FREDDIE: I think it comes from reaching a point in my life and realizing that my priorities were all out of whack. My mom worked at Walgreen's for 12 years, and after 12 years, I think she was making $8 an hour. And there I was, a millionaire living in a penthouse suite in Florida, and seeing her a couple times a year. I had the house, the cars, the stuff – but it was all wrong. And one of the things I've learned now, after having everything and losing it, is that the biggest "thing" in life is not a "thing" at all.

When the cars, the houses, and the stuff are all gone, it really is about who you have been able to associate yourself with, and what legacy you are leaving as you leave this planet. I didn't like the legacy I

143

was leaving at all. When all that happened, the people that I thought were my friends were nowhere to be found. I was really kind of mad about it all. But then I looked at how many people's lives I had affected. I asked myself, "had I had a positive or negative impact?" I know in some ways, there were some positives, but in many other areas of my life, there were many negatives. I knew that I was reaping many of the negative seeds that I had sown.

When you do see somebody in need, don't question how they are going to use the money, or whether or not they are going to use it for food. You can do your part by giving it to them and trusting that they're going to do what they should be doing with it, versus the unseen, you know the scepticism or the cynical thoughts that you may have that they are just going to waste it. We all deserve a second chance. "Paying it forward" really resonates with what I want others to see in me now, versus that person I was in the past. I want a person to see someone that has a good heart and that his actions speak louder than words. They don't have to know it, but hopefully, they will be able to feel it—it's not about the money.

SCOTT: And that carries through for your wife, Mitzi, as well.

FREDDIE: That's really where I learned a lot of it, from HER. She's a very giving person! I don't know who in their right mind would literally turn over their life savings to somebody, and when it's gone, how would you feel? How do you handle that? How do you deal with all that emotional stuff that she had to be going through? She always stuck with me through thick and thin. I was the one to say let's hoard it, let's keep it. We need this to pay the bills. We need this to make ends meet. She said well, we've got to do our part to be right about this. We've got to give it away, we've got to tithe. We've got to do the stuff that it looks like we can't do, because, only then can we exercise our faith. It was an amazing thing when an IRS check showed up in the mail as a refund. We didn't pay taxes, and it arrived the very day that we desperately needed it. God works in His time.

If you just follow the rules of the Good Book, it kind of lays it out there. Mitzi had that foundation, that upbringing, and she is this kind of person that I strive to be.

SCOTT: That's awesome! Are there any particular organizations that you and Mitzi support that you would suggest support of?

FREDDIE: First of all, we're strong believers in helping to educate the average person to get control of their finances—not just in the stock market but also in other areas of their finances, for example, showing people that they can pay off their mortgage in 15 years instead of 20 years by just making one additional payment to the principle every year, making 13 payments instead of 12—becoming financially literate, if you will.

But even more importantly, we feel, is the support that we give to the Gideons organization. The Gideons are responsible for giving out Bibles to people all over the country and various parts of the world and are also responsible for placing the Bibles in hotel rooms.

We have also been supporters of an organization who trains world leaders in the Gospel to allow them to better spread the Gospel to people of their own cultures. This organization is Haggai Institute.

In addition to this, we also enjoy contributing to local people who have had the opportunity to travel to India to minister to many people in that area of the world.

We have been supporters of the Joyce Meyer Ministry. She is no doubt, in our opinion, one of the greatest teachers in practical living that has ever existed. Her teachings have helped Mitzi and myself tremendously.

We are also supporters of gospel music. We have been able to help local talent, as well as national talent in that arena.

One of the most rewarding areas is helping with various needs that occur in our small community in which we live. We always try to help with those individual needs when the opportunity presents itself. This is an area that I would encourage everyone to participate. It is of the utmost importance that we help those around us when needed, and, like I said, is most rewarding.

SCOTT: Those are great. Do you have any one last lesson that you would like to pass along?

FREDDIE: I would just say, "Do what you love and the money will follow. Make your vocation a vacation. And pay it forward". That's a big belief that I have. Let's not worry about paying it back, but if we can

145

pay it forward and have others do the same, it would make this world a better place, and the rewards will be beyond your wildest dreams.

SCOTT: Thank you very much.

- To help support The Gideons International, obtain information and make donations, go to www.gideons.org, or call (615) 564-5000.
- To reach Freddie, contact him at www.BetterTrades.com.
- To help support the Joyce Meyer Ministries and make donations, please contact http://joycemeyer.org, or call 800-727-9673.
- To help support the Haggai Institute and make donations, please contact http://haggai-institute.com.

Niki Curry
Entrepreneur with a Heart for Helping

As a successful entrepreneur across multiple industries, Niki has sought out and studied with many of the most successful mentors in their respective areas of expertise. She in turn has turned that knowledge into multiple successful systems and businesses herself. More importantly, what motivates her is the compelling plight and opportunity of improving the lives of orphans worldwide. She is an empowering and compassionate woman with her heart set on service.

SCOTT: Niki, you are truly amazing. Give us some insight into your vast experience in both real estate and the Internet.

NIKI: I am a very proud native Texan. I believe my upbringing helped me be where I am right now. Currently, I have a number of companies; one is a private investment firm that I am President and CSO, or as I call it "Chief Servant Officer." We invest in real estate, tax liens and privately held real estate notes. The company started because of an individual in Los Angeles wanting me to help him find privately held real estate notes. He would pay me a commission and I was blown away at how much he was willing to pay me. I decided to learn more to find out how much he was earning. In doing so, it morphed into a company and then expanded into the different areas. I have a penchant for learning so if I like something, I would go and find a way to accelerate it.

Another company is an international Internet company which is the one I am *the* most proud out of because it came out of a *deep* desire to help orphan children around the world.

SCOTT: That's pretty cool. How did you jump from using your expertise in real estate into an international Internet business?

NIKI: I had a beautiful upbringing and a very strong mentor in my granddaddy. He always thought big and he kept instilling in me, "Don't think big things—*do* big things!" Many times, I found myself almost like a fish out of water growing up because my friends were not thinking that way. As I was growing up I found myself gravitating more to that mind set because he was so inspirational and was such a strong mentor. Going

147

into another business, especially to help orphans, in my opinion was "doing big things!"

SCOTT: How did that lead to your desire to help orphans?

NIKI: Several years ago I went on a mission trip in Mexico and volunteered in an orphanage. I saw firsthand the plight of this orphanage, the orphans, and the deplorable conditions they were living in. I also fell in love with a courageous little boy named Pepe. I felt I needed to do more.

During this time frame, I had wanted to adopt and was looking into international adoption. The red tape and all the things that were clouding this process were amazing. It's not as easy of a process like we're led to believe in Hollywood. It was that desire of doing something more for these children, who often times were abandoned by their own parents, living on the streets and yet, they did not have a voice. It was awful so I made the decision to do more and help them.

At the time two of my very close mentors, Mark Victor Hansen and Bob Allen were doing a seminar called "Cracking the Millionaire Code." I had been a protégé of theirs years prior. They originally helped me become a millionaire. I went to their workshop in San Diego in February of 2005. There was a presentation by a speaker selling things over the Internet to his current database. A friend of mine was also talking about selling an E-book on eBay. She made twelve thousand dollars over in the course of the weekend and I thought, "Oh my gosh— she's here at this event, she's making twelve grand on the Internet, using eBay as her marketplace!" I was just blown away.

Then came speaker, Jay Abraham talking about joint ventures, selling other peoples' materials if they didn't have your own products or books, which I didn't. He explained you could joint venture with other people and market their products for them earning a handsome commission. On the drive back to my home in Southern California, I was so jazzed and motivated because of connecting those three dots—the database, the Internet, and joint ventures—with the possibilities.

It became my personal strategy to earning additional income to donate to the orphans. I never really thought it was ever going to morph into where it is today. The whole business moved forward because of my passion to help these precious orphaned children. If you saw their little faces and the places where they live as I have, you would understand more.

SCOTT: Amazing—you entered into an arena that you really had no expertise in. You heard the idea and went out to seek that expertise?

NIKI: I had learned enough from that workshop, and the Internet is interesting enough that it's not hard to get started. After seeing some results, the recognition came to seek wisdom from people who were already achieving success in that same arena. That's been my life philosophy. If you want to be successful, don't listen to just anybody, don't buy just anybody's tapes, don't go to just anybody's workshops. Go to the people who are in the position financially you desire or have achieved what you want to achieve and learn.

That position could be miles apart from where you are now but you need to learn from the best. Seek out wisdom and other people's expertise. Then hone the information from all these different sources and condense it into your own.

I was already running another company; my time was at a premium and so I figured that I needed to condense all this information into a simpler, yet effective and successful plan to continue to support these orphans.

SCOTT: Out of your desire to help orphans worldwide, your Internet business was born?

NIKI: Yes, absolutely—and thriving. I love the result—not because of what it is doing for me and my lifestyle but because all net proceeds go to help the orphans. I love it because it's my passion. I am so blessed that I found the passion that I am really focused on and its helping these orphans around the world. We also help some families get the opportunity to adopt and bring these children home. I know I am doing something to contribute to an innocent person's life out of gratitude for what I have been blessed with personally and professionally.

SCOTT: What was the challenge put forth by one of your mentors that resulted in an entirely new product you developed?

NIKI: I have a very competitive spirit—I learned that from my grand-daddy. As a protégé of Mark Victor Hansen and Bob Allen, and a member of their millionaire hall of fame, I was being invited to go to New York to help to promote the book *Cracking the Millionaire Code*. We were going to be on television and radio with all this media attention surrounding the book launch. I wanted to personally create a new success story before the launch. The internal pressure was on me from February to the first part of June because that's when we were going to New York as a group.

I told myself that I was going to earn six figures in this new enterprise between February 28 and June 1. That was my goal. I didn't know how it was going to happen because again I didn't have access to any of these people who were on the platform from the "Cracking the Millionaire Code" workshop but I had the desire; I had enough knowledge and know how to go after the right people.

To make a long story short I accomplished making six figures and it only took forty five days! Hence my program now is called "Six Figures in Forty Five Days.com."

SCOTT: What's the driving force behind that program?

NIKI: I had spent about sixty grand going to seminars and workshops to learn from the experts. They were the best of the best—the ones who had a certain pinnacle of success that I was looking to achieve. The investment was made to learn from them collectively so that I could refine it into layman's terms. Not being an Internet guru at the time, I had to break it down to nuts and bolts, how I could understand it and hand it off to a new comer.

All the information was put together so that it was easy to understand and very concise. More importantly, somebody didn't have to spend sixty grand and take the time I did to learn. They could really get on the Internet; they could create their database—the goal of this program. After all, if you have a database and it's consistently growing, you can sell from that database over and over and over again. That's how the revenue is generated.

SCOTT: That's pretty exciting. As you created "Six Figures," your real desire was to help others be able to change their position in life so that they can help more people as well?

NIKI: Oh, absolutely, I believe that we are all eligible to live in the world of abundance. And I say eligible because I believe that God wants us to have an abundant life. Typically, what stops us is ourselves, our mind set, our history, or the naysayers in our life. "Six Figures" was designed to affordably help people get out of the box they were in by getting into an industry where research and all the indicators say is the place to be—the Internet. With their success, they can help others by paying it forward.

SCOTT: That's exciting. In helping others achieve wealth and freedom in their lives, your real desire is to get them to be able to support whatever it is in their life they want to support.

NIKI: Absolutely—imagine if even ten people were able to donate a thousand dollars each and every single month. That's ten thousand dollars into helping somebody on this planet. It doesn't matter what the charity was; that could be the only donation they ever make to that one charity, but that money or the resources or their time can be leveraged and help even more people. It's just amazing!

There is an organization that I support that provides surgeries for children that have cleft palates. Ultimately, the donation is small but can you imagine what we're actually doing for that one child to have that surgery. It's a few thousand dollars. They have instant, I don't know—what's the word I'm looking for?

SCOTT: Self-esteem change?

NIKI: Self-esteem, exactly—they're no longer looked at differently and they can accomplish all kinds of things that will be passed forward to another generation. Maybe they just become a point of encouragement to somebody who has a cleft palate. By sharing their story another, may not give up and maintain hope.

SCOTT: While you have this ongoing real estate and investment business which allows you to live a very comfortable and fruitful life, it's really the Internet businesses that you are excited about to reach your true passions?

NIKI: You know, that's funny, because when I am hearing you ask the question I never really looked at it that way. You're absolutely right. I believe that we originally crave to satisfy our needs and even some wants, and there's nothing wrong with that. However, when you get past all the toys, then it's no longer about you and your life. After all, how many homes can you have? And how much jewelry can you really buy yourself? The realization is when your life and my life have changed focus into "What can I do for somebody else? How can I lift somebody else up today? What can I give to leave a legacy so that whatever I am creating and whatever I am being blessed with can be used long after I am gone from this Earth"?

SCOTT: Fascinating—why is that so important to you?

NIKI: For several reasons, once again because of my mentor, my granddaddy. I feel like this is my way of saying I got the message. Secondly, it's important to me because I believe that my life will ultimately glorify God and my walk with Him is extremely important. And thirdly, I believe that I was given these talents, gifts, and abilities and put on this Earth to do great things.

My granddaddy used to tell me to look at my life and ask the question "Is your life a book worth reading?" I want my life to be worth reading to hopefully inspire somebody else when I am gone.

SCOTT: That's a great way of putting it and an inspiration to so many who will read this. How do we make our lives worth reading?

NIKI: First, it's a mind set. I have probably spent just as much, if not, more money on self development. In fact, I was at my sister's over the weekend and we were exchanging books. She reads novels and I read self-help and how-to type books. She asked me the question, "Why do you search for information and knowledge instead of just relaxing and reading a novel?"

I do relax and read novels but this life is so short that I believe that somebody could really just work on themselves. There is so much information out there. To change their mind set and to let them know that they are worth it. That they deserve it and they can have it all if they choose to take action and ask God for *His* help and direction.

SCOTT: How do we convey that message to so many more?

NIKI: Through a platform like you are doing with *Talking With Giants!*^TM If somebody is really searching, they are going to go to the bookstore or to the library and they're going to find what they are looking for because when they are ready, the material or people they need to meet just appears; it's "magic!"

With the advent of the Internet and all the teleclasses and the Webinars, it's making it so much more affordable for people to learn. After all, not everybody has sixty thousand dollars and time off from work to go and search for this information out like I did to be earning the type of income I have been blessed to generate. With the Webinars and teleseminars, and books, it now becomes very affordable. This is especially true for single parents for example. They don't have to travel and leave their kids with a baby sitter. In the comfort of their home they can tap into this information from their computer. These days, there is really no excuse not to change your lives if they really, really want it badly enough.

SCOTT: That's really true. The driving force behind *Talking With Giants!*^TM is to grow awareness and really get people to understand that we all have so much to give.

NIKI: Absolutely, and the funny thing is, you shouldn't give *when* you think you've reached a certain pinnacle of success, you should start now wherever you are. If it's even volunteering one hour a month, you are still giving, aren't you?

SCOTT: Absolutely, give of your time and talents.

NIKI: That's right! If you can give one dollar a month, I can assure you that first dollar is probably the best dollar you've ever given. And that start brings so much self satisfaction. You start changing your mind set and the way you see things. It's stunning that when you give, opportunities appear, people enter your life, and good things just start happening. It's almost like a miracle. It's truly "magical." I dare people to test it for themselves and see for themselves.

SCOTT: Well, it truly is something as small as a little additional tip or just even a smile or a kind word.

NIKI: Absolutely, what about a hug? You know how many people want to be touched?

SCOTT: That's very true; it doesn't take all that much, does it?

NIKI: No, it's a mind set.

SCOTT: What helped you gain that mind set the most?

NIKI: This is interesting because I am really an introvert. I am very shy and very private. Then again, because of my upbringing in Texas, you know we have a slogan there that says, "Texas friendly" and that was a big, huge influence for me and then my granddaddy. I saw my granddaddy reach out to people who worked on his ranch. He didn't care that they were his employees, he didn't care that they were not the owner or a manager or a supervisor. All he did was just love them.

If all he had was beans and a chicken, that's what he offered them. I really learned by example. From my beautiful parents too! They just gave and gave and gave to us. How can you not learn something from beautiful people you are surrounded with?

SCOTT: That's absolutely true. So another key is surrounding yourself with the best of the best?

NIKI: Absolutely I am very blessed to have had the lessons of purging myself from people who no longer fit where you wanted to go. That may sound harsh and cruel. But is it? By staying in those relationships, you stay at a level that you didn't want to be. If you want to reach out and be living at a higher level of abundance to help more people, the people who are not of like mind really need to be purged. Then go search for the other people you want to be living among in this life of abundance.

When you live from the place of abundance, with people who are like-minded, they encourage and lift you up. They help you soar and fly in higher places than you never dreamed about.

SCOTT: In fairness to the people you separate from, it actually frees them to go off and have a more fruitful, more on purpose life as well, wouldn't you agree?

NIKI: If they choose to, they can also stay there. One of my favorite sayings is: don't complain about something unless you're willing to do something about it. That was a very important lesson to me because we can all complain about our circumstances, but what are we going to do about it?

SCOTT: Very true. Without action nothing changes.

NIKI: Absolutely, and we have that choice every single day.

SCOTT: Are there any things that cause you to make those choices or is it something now that is just so ingrained?

NIKI: No, you know it's a struggle. Just because I live in this world of abundance doesn't mean that it is easy to be here, you know I go through the same struggles and challenges like everybody else. The difference is that when I find myself going to a lower level, I have to do something to bring myself back up quickly.

    I love being outside in nature. I go for little mini walks, I'll go play with my dog, I'll pick up the phone and call my mother, sister, or best friend, S.J. There are all kinds of things that you can do to bring yourself up where you need to be. I even listen to Les Brown; he's got this little promotional video. I think it is about ninety seconds long. You can listen to it over and over and over again.

    While listening to it I am thinking, "wow—I need to get "back up" because I am not going to do anything productive like this in my present mind set."

SCOTT: That's awesome! It's amazing how much we can do not only for ourselves but for so many others if we keep ourselves in that place.

NIKI: Absolutely, it's a challenge. It does take work, but it is worth it!

SCOTT: Tell us a little bit more about the orphans. Is there a foundation that you support?

NIKI: Yes, it is my own private foundation. I chose that entity because I wanted my giving to be anonymous. The foundation gives to all kinds of organizations including the one which helps children have surgeries for cleft palates. Whatever I can do that helps orphaned children around the world—we look into it.

SCOTT: Are there any public charities that you'd like to see supported through these efforts at *Talking With Giants!*™?

NIKI: Yes, I really like Shaohannah's Hope, a Christian organization that helps families that want to adopt internationally. It was started by Steven Curtis Chapman, a Dove Award-winner. He and his wife have adopted internationally. I really, really, love what they are all about.

There are enough caring couples desiring to adopt to support the orphanages around the world. Often times when you adopt you are also contributing back to those orphanages. Shaohannah's Hope, as a Christian organization even helps with financial support in some cases. Adoption is very expensive—international adoption is up to thirty and sometimes forty thousand dollars when it's all said and done.

It is not fair but many of the adoption attorneys in third world countries know that Americans have money and will spend it to adopt a child. So it's expensive. And yet, Shaohanna's Hope has a plethora of resources to help a family that is considering adoption. This is the one organization that would encompass everything that I believe in working with in the arena of adoption.

SCOTT: That's great. Is there one last suggestion that you would like to share with everybody?

NIKI: Two things: one, do whatever you can to work on yourself for personal growth and don't stop. Second is: choose the mentor you want to follow and follow him or her. Had I not had the mentors in Mark and Bob I probably would not have been on the Internet right now.

The Internet is hot, it is easy, and it's something you can do alongside with what you're already doing. It is just a marvelous, marvelous industry to go into especially because of the way it is positioned in the market place. The Internet may not be for everybody, so whatever you do just follow the mentors that you respect and want to follow because they are in the place you want to be in both integrity wise and financially too!

One more thing, start giving today—even if it is one hour, one hug, or one dollar—we *all* can make a difference!

SCOTT: Great words of wisdom there, for sure. Love it, that's awesome. Thank you for giving us some great insights!

- To help support Shaohannah's Hope, obtain information and make donations, please contact http://www.shaohannahshope.org, or call 615-550-5600.
- To obtain more information on how Niki has been so successful creating over a 1m database and Internet success of her own, please visit http://6Figuresin45Days.com
- To learn more about Niki—Author, Investor, Infopreneur, Philanthropist, please visit http://NikiCurry.com.

Invitation for Support and Giving

"Think of an idea to change our world. And put it into action," was an invitation given to the actors in the movie, *Pay It Forward,* released in 2000. *Pay It Forward* proposes that if we help people do something they can't do for themselves, and they then turn around and do it for three other people, we might just change the world!

Each of the charities and organizations discussed in *Talking with Giants!*™ is doing amazing work to help those in need! As blessed as we all are, we have been given talents and abilities far beyond those of so many people. In my view, by the very fact that you are reading this book—you are a *Giant!* You are seriously looking at contributing more to humanity. You should be applauded for your efforts to date.

With that comes a natural and urgent Invitation for Support and Giving. Please, I urge those reading this book to use the talents and abilities you have already been given to support and help others. Your support can come through financial means, donating time, wisdom, or even your talents to help those in need.

Hopefully, your support comes in alignment with one of the groups listed below. If not these, please find someone or some organization that you can invest in on a consistent basis. Thank you in advance for your interest and enthusiasm, and please—

Pay It Forward!

- To help support **Abundant Life Ranch**, obtain information and make donations, go to www.abundantliferanch.org, or call 816-721-0608.
- To help support **Achilles Track Club**, obtain information and make donations, please contact www.Achillestrackclub.org, or call 212-354-0300.
- To help support the **American Red Cross**, obtain information and make donations, go to www.redcross.org, or call 800-REDCROSS.
- To help support the **Autism Society**, obtain information and make donations, please contact www.autism-society.org, or call 1-800-3 AUTISM.

- To help support **BeSomeone**, obtain information and make donations, please contact http://www.BeSomeone.org, or call 678-526-0292.
- To help support the **Boys Clubs and Girls Clubs**, obtain information and make donations, go to www.bgca.org, or call 404-487-5700.
- To help support **CALM**, obtain information and make donations, please contact http://calm4kids.org, or call 805-965-2376.
- To help support **Fellowship Church**, obtain information and make donations, go to www.fellowshipchurch.com, or call 972-471-5700. You can drop by and visit at 2450 Highway 121 North, Grapevine, Texas 76051.
- To help support **The Gideons International**, obtain information and make donations, go to www.gideons.org, or call (615) 564-5000.
- To help support **Habitat for Humanity**, obtain information and make donations, go to www.habitat.org, or call 229-924-6935.
- To help support the **Haggai Institute** and make donations, please contact http://haggai-institute.com.
- To help support the **Joyce Meyers Ministries** and make donations, please contact http://joycemeyer.org, or call 800-727-9673.
- To help support the **Juvenile Diabetes Foundation International**, obtain information and make donations, go to www.jdrf.org, or call 1-800-JDF-CURE. You can also e-mail the Dallas Chapter at dallas@jdrf.org.
- To support the **Park Avenue Christian School**, obtain information and make donations, please contact http://pacschool.org, or call 417-865-9875.
- To help support **Parker College of Chiropractic**, obtain information and make donations, go to www.parkercc.edu, or call 972-438-6932.
- To help support **ProLiteracy Worldwide**, obtain information and make donations, please contact http://www.proliteracy.org, or call Toll Free: 888-528-2224.
- To help support **Shaohannah's Hope**, obtain information and make donations, please contact http://www.shaohannahshope.org or call: 615-550-5600.

- To help support **SPCA**, obtain information and make donations, please contact http://SPCA.com.
- To help support **Triage**, obtain information and make donations, go to www.Triage.ca, or call 604-254-3700.
- To help support the **United Way**, obtain information and make donations, go to http://national.unitedway.org, or call 214-978-0000.
- To support the **Unstoppable Foundation**, obtain information and make donations, please contact: http://unstoppable.net/foundation.asp, or call 888-867-8677.

Thank you for who you are—and your desire to help others!

About the Author

After spending more than thirty years in the sales, marketing, training, management, and speaking arenas, Scott is uniquely qualified to help individuals and organizations achieve the success they desire. With vast experience over a range of industries, Scott's value-added conceptual expertise in all aspects of business shouts out loud and clear.

While going to the University of Iowa on a football scholarship, Scott became a licensed life insurance agent at the age of eighteen. In his first month in business, Scott sold over a quarter million dollars worth of insurance. It's not hard to understand that with the years of personal selling background he has embodied, armed with a Bachelor of Business Administration degree with majors in marketing and insurance, Scott possesses the expertise necessary to educate, empower, and inspire others to achieve "their" success.

Since his years at Iowa, Scott has worked for and with Fortune 500 companies and individuals, growing and sharing his expertise. When it comes to understanding the opportunity at hand, there are few others that can grasp the issues, diagnose the problems, design the remedy, and implement the cure as well.

As an Internationally acclaimed Speaker, Author and Success Expert, Scott has lead the field in training others, presenting as a top professional speaker and executing the very success strategies he teaches.

- To order additional copies of *Talking With Giants!*[TM] for fund raising, corporate events, training or promotions, please visit www.talkingwithgiants.com.
- To book Scott for your next corporate event, or to inquire about consulting services, please call 972.659.8941 or e-mail scott@scottschilling.com.
- To learn more about Scott, please visit www.scottschilling.com.